THINKING
ABOUT
PROGRAM
EVALUATION

2

THINKING
ABOUT
PROGRAM
EVALUATION
2

WITHDRAWN

RICHARD A. BERK
PETER H. ROSSI

SAGE Publications
International Educational and Professional Publisher
Thousand Oaks London New Delhi

7989162

KSG - API 206

Copyright © 1999 by Sage Publications, Inc.

For information:

SAGE Publications, Inc.
2455 Teller Road
Thousand Oaks, California 91320
E-mail: order@sagepub.com

SAGE Publications Ltd.
6 Bonhill Street
London EC2A 4PU
United Kingdom

SAGE Publications India Pvt. Ltd.
M-32 Market
Greater Kailash I
New Delhi 110 048 India

Printed in the United States of America

Library of Congress Cataloging-in-Publication Data

Berk, Richard A.
    Thinking about program evaluation / by Richard A. Berk and Peter H. Rossi.—2nd ed.
        p. cm.
    Includes bibliographical references and index.
    ISBN 0-7619-1764-0 (cloth: acid-free paper)
    ISBN 0-7619-1765-9 (pbk.: acid-free paper)
    1. Evaluation research (Social action programs)—Utilization.
    I. Rossi, Peter Henry, 1921- II. Title.
    H62.B428   1998
    361.6'068—ddc21   98-25412

        03 04 05 7 6 5 4

Acquiring Editor:	C. Deborah Laughton
Editorial Assistant:	Eileen Carr
Production Editor:	Diana E. Axelsen
Editorial Assistant:	Denise Santoyo
Typesetter/Designer:	Lynn Miyata
Indexer:	Virgil Diodato
Cover Designer:	Candice Harman

Contents

Prologue

Although the field of evaluation research has not changed dramatically since the first edition, the number of evaluation studies completed has been enormous. Many of these newer efforts reflect continually evolving policy concerns and the importation of some recent statistical technology. Thus, in this second edition, we have taken great pains to provide the most recent references to both substantive and methodological work and, at the same time, we have retained the best older studies, some undertaken more than a generation ago.

Our thinking has not changed dramatically since the first edition, although we would like to believe it has not stagnated either. Readers will find somewhat more complete discussions of methodological issues and the introduction of several new topics: meta-analysis, selection models, instrumental variable estimation, and others. Practical concerns are informed by another decade of hands-on experience both authors have had doing evaluation research. And insofar as aging fosters perspective, that, too, will be reflected in the text.

Finally, since the first edition, evaluation research has lost two of its pioneers and finest practitioners: Donald Campbell and Howard Freeman. Both were colleagues and friends. Both are missed.

Nostra Cupla[1]

In the preparation of this edition, we came across several paragraphs in the first edition that were virtually identical to paragraphs in the fifth edition of Rossi and Freedman's *Evaluation: A Systematic Approach*. We suspect that in this world of modern word processors, some all-too-hasty cutting and pasting inadvertently produced this result. We apologize.

Note

1. Thanks go to Rachel V. Berk, and indirectly to the Santa Barbara, California, Junior High School, for the Latin translation of "our guilt."

1

What This Book Is About

What Is Evaluation Research?

Program evaluation derives from the commonsense idea that social programs should have demonstrable benefits. Literacy programs for adults, for example, should lead to measurable improvements in reading skills. Lowering speed limits on interstate highways should significantly reduce the number of automobile fatalities and save gasoline. Increasing the length of prison sentences for white-collar criminals should clearly reduce the amount of insider trading. Increasing the price of electricity during the middle of the day should visibly reduce consumption during "peak-load" hours. Efforts to educate sexually active individuals about "safe sex" should plainly slow the spread of AIDS. Implicit is the notion that social programs ought to have explicit aims by which success or failure may be empirically judged. Mere assertions about success or failure are insufficient. The assertions must be supported by evidence.

It should not be surprising, therefore, that program evaluation, broadly construed, has a very long history. Hunters and gatherers thousands of years ago, for example, developed complicated communal procedures for flushing and trapping game based on the size of the catch and the danger involved. In ancient Rome, tax policies were altered in response to observed fluctuations in revenues. During the last decades of the eighteenth century, the British Admiralty began requiring that its crews eat citrus fruits on long voyages after evidence was produced showing that consuming these fruits prevented scurvy. Early in the twentieth century, the indeterminate prison sentence was introduced in the United States, partly in response to the high rates of recidivism under earlier sentencing policies. In short, judgments have always been made about whether prospective or ongoing programs were effective.

In recent years, however, commonsense program evaluation has evolved into *evaluation research,* a heterogeneous mix of substantive issues and procedures of considerable sophistication and power. Evaluation research includes the design of social programs, the ongoing monitoring of how well programs are functioning, the assessment of program impact, and the analysis of the program benefits relative to their costs. In addition, the traditional literature review has of late evolved into a formal procedure called *meta-analysis,* which attempts to provide estimates of program impact by combining the findings from a number of distinct evaluations. Thus, one might inquire whether a particular job training program is reaching the people most in need of help (i.e., a monitoring question) and then whether the training demonstrably leads to greater success in the labor market (i.e., an impact question). Meanwhile, one might also try to estimate the average impact of similar job training programs in the past (i.e., a meta-analysis) by summarizing systematically the findings of many evaluations.

Evaluation research necessarily employs a variety of research methods: ethnography, survey research, randomized experiments, benefit-cost analysis, and others. A variety of methods are used because different methods have different strengths and weaknesses, and because the particular questions being asked should be coupled with the most effective research methods. For instance, in designing a program, it is always important to know what the target population is. The size and nature of the target population usually are best determined by survey procedures.

Finally, evaluation research capitalizes on existing theory and empirical generalizations from the social sciences. Understanding of why a particular water or energy conservation plan failed (or succeeded), for instance, might be greatly enhanced by insights from both microeconomics and social psychology. Likewise, a lot might be learned from sociology and psychology about how to devise programs to reduce teenage pregnancy. Yet such advances would be irrelevant without the interest and support of policymakers and other interested parties who believe that social programs should be held accountable and that evaluation research can provide empirical evidence about program accountability. That is, without interest in *and* funding from organizations or agencies who have a stake in whether a particular program is working, evaluation research would soon wither away.

At its best, however, evaluation research can only help policymakers and interested parties make judgments about the relative success or failure of programs and policies, whether these be prospective or in operation. Evaluation research is *not* a substitute for judgments by policymakers, and responsible evaluators should have no interest in either circumventing the political process or becoming de facto policymakers themselves. Put another way, evaluation research is essentially about providing the most accurate information practically possible in an evenhanded manner. For example, an evaluation study might determine the likely impact of a program providing information about sexually transmitted diseases to adolescent schoolchildren but leave unaddressed the political question of whether the schools should make such programs mandatory. An evaluation might estimate the degree to which charges for the treatment of wastewater would deter manufacturers from polluting but be silent on the fairness of such pricing policies. Or an evaluation might determine that bottle-ban initiatives really reduce litter but take no position on whether such bans are an unreasonable interference with a free market.

What, then, is distinctive about evaluation research? How is it different from newspaper reporting or social commentary? How is it different from social science more broadly? Evaluation research differs from newspaper reporting and social commentary by relying on the scientific method. Although reporters or social observers certainly depend in part on empirical information, their work is not scrutinized by the scientific community and is not held to the same standards of evidence. There is, for instance, no requirement of replicability; there is no requirement that other investigators independently produce the same results. Evaluation research differs from the social sciences in its goals and audience. Rather than having the policy community as its most direct and important audience, social science has social scientists as its most direct and important audience. The goal is to advance social theory, or at least empirical generalizations about the social world.

At the same time, the lines between evaluation research and a number of other policy-related enterprises are not always clear-cut. Perhaps the best example is policy analysis, which shares much with evaluation research but also offers advice to stakeholders about how to analyze and construct social policies. For example, policy analysis often takes as given some social attribute to optimize, such as efficiency, and then uses theory from economics or operations research tells stakeholders what they *should* do. Alternatively, current policies may be judged using the efficient ideal as a benchmark. Thus, there has been a lot of effort recently to develop policies for the optimal regulation of greenhouse gases, which scientists increasingly believe lead to global climate change (Office of Science and Technology 1997). On the one hand, there needs to be a reduction of greenhouse gas emissions, primarily carbon dioxide produced by the burning of fossil fuels and by deforestation. On the other hand, the possible economic damage from those reductions should be minimized (Nordhaus 1994). If such a plan were developed, it could be the "gold standard" with which to compare current policies or be the recommended policy for the future. Other applications of policy analysis include optimal drug enforcement policies, efficient use of police patrol cars, effective copayments for managed heath care, and sustainable fishing practices. In each case, the emphasis is on how to properly conceptualize particular social policies.

It is also sometimes important to appreciate that evaluation research may be conducted by people who do not consciously identify their work as such. The recent concerns about global climate change, for instance, have been in part informed by large-scale computer simulations representing the impact of greenhouse gases on global climate (Intergovernmental Panel on Climate Change 1997). These computer models allow scientists to do "experiments" in which the climate impact of different hypothetical levels of greenhouse gases may be projected. That is, the scientists can, within the limits of their models, determine what the climate would be like under different greenhouse gas scenarios. Because the scenarios depend on human activities, the scientists are able to evaluate prospectively the impact of various policies to limit the production of greenhouse gases. These evaluations, in turn, have been central in a number of formal discussions between diplomats from around the world. By almost any definition, this is evaluation research. Yet much of the work is done by scientists who see themselves doing basic research on climate. The general point is that evaluation research should be defined by its content and goals and not necessarily by its label.

What Is Good Evaluation Research?

So what is a *successful* evaluation? To anticipate a bit, an evaluation attains *practical* perfection when it provides the best information possible on the key policy questions within the given set of real-world constraints. This implies that *all* evaluations are flawed if measured against the yardstick of abstract perfection or if judged without taking time, budget, ethical, and political restrictions into account. In other words, there is really no such thing as a truly perfect evaluation, and idealized textbook treatments of research design and analysis typically establish useful aspirations but unrealistic expectations. An instructive example is a recent evaluation of managed mental health services (*American Psychologist* 1997; Bickman et al. 1995), in which the findings do not confirm conventional wisdom that managed mental health services lead to better mental health outcomes and lower costs, compared to the usual manner in which health care services are delivered. Although the authors themselves stress that the study was far from textbook-perfect, many commentators believe with Sechrest and Walsh (1997, 536) that "it is difficult to imagine that a better study of anywhere near equivalent scope will be done soon, if ever."

A "merely" successful evaluation, in contrast, falls short of providing the best information possible under the given circumstances but provides better information than would otherwise have been available. That is, the proper measure of success is adding to current knowledge, not what ultimately might be good to know. Thus, if very little is known about the effectiveness of a particular program, an evaluation that would rate as weak on a pure methodological scale may nevertheless be an enormous success in practice. The work on global warming briefly described previously is one instance. Current efforts to evaluate the possible impact of "carbon taxes" (e.g., adding a new 5-cent tax to each gallon of gasoline sold) on fossil fuel consumption are extremely crude. But they are very valuable and influential because at this time we know so little.

Note that nothing is being said about how the evaluation is ultimately used. Indeed, an evaluation may be successful even if the information provided is ignored, or even misused. Once the findings are presented in a clear and accessible fashion, the evaluation is over. What follows is certainly critical, but it is essentially a political process. Interested evaluators are best off observing the action at some distance, preferably through safety glasses.

Our position on what is successful evaluation research is not universally accepted in the evaluation community. There are some self-identified evaluation researchers who take the position that successful evaluation research must include an advocacy component. Continuing with the global warming example, these researchers maintain that the evaluator should use the information from the research to take public positions on the issues—in other words, the evaluator should actively take sides. Although advocacy is certainly an important enterprise, it is a risky endeavor for evaluation researchers. The pitfalls are many, but perhaps most important, the credibility of the research can be seriously undermined. If the evaluation researcher is known to be an advocate for a particular side, questions can always be raised about how evenhanded the research really is. And even the "appearance of impropriety" may be devastating in how the work is received.

There are other evaluators who believe that a successful evaluation is one that is actually used by policymakers or by program managers (Cronbach 1982; Patton 1997). Although we certainly agree that how evaluation research results are used is important, we worry about employing those concerns as a yardstick for evaluation research. One problem is the determination of who the users really will be, and accidentally identifying one group of users at the expense of others risks the appearance of advocacy. One can easily imagine the problems that might follow if an evaluation of carbon taxes is deemed successful because it is used by oil companies even though it is ignored by conservation groups. Moreover, the advocacy may become real if an evaluator succumbs to the temptation to cater to the stakeholders who have clear investments in the worth of the program being evaluated. In short, it is important to be responsive to the evaluation questions raised by stakeholders and to provide accurate and accessible accounts of the findings. But in our view, an evaluation can be successful even if ignored or misused by stakeholders.

Goals and Organization of This Book

This book provides an introduction to the variety of purposes for which evaluation research may be used and to the range of methods that are currently employed. Specific examples are given to provide concrete illustrations of both the goals of evaluation research and the methods applied. Although the book is intended to be comprehensive in the sense of describing major uses of evaluation research, it cannot pretend to be encyclopedic.

We want to be especially clear, therefore, on what this book is *not*. The book is not remotely detailed enough or technical enough to prepare the reader to do credible evaluation research. For the same reasons, it will not prepare the reader to develop new evaluation research methods or philosophies. But to those ends, citations to more detailed discussions are provided, including citations to statistical references. In addition, we strongly encourage the reader to consult surveys of the field (Cook and Campbell 1979; Cronbach 1982; Cronbach and Associates 1980; Guba and Lincoln 1981; Guttentag and Struening 1975; Rossi and Freeman 1993; Suchman 1967; Weiss 1972, 1997) and broad methodological discussions that can be very instructive, even though not focused specifically on evaluation research (Cochran 1983; Kish 1987; Rosenbaum 1995).

The book is consciously designed to address central ideas within two formats. First, key concepts are briefly introduced, in part as a kind of dictionary for later discussions. The goal is to acquaint the reader with a few fundamental ideas. Second, the evaluation research enterprise is presented in an idealized, chronological fashion to emphasize that the research methods employed depend on the question being asked and the stage of the evolution of the social program under scrutiny. For example, research procedures that might well make sense as a program is initially being designed may be irrelevant when the impact of an ongoing program is being addressed. Likewise, research procedures that are effective in determining *how* a program works will often differ from research procedures that are effective in determining *whether* a program works. In short, our message is pragmatic; research tools should be chosen for the particular job at hand.

2

Key Concepts
in Evaluation Research

We turn initially to a number of central concepts in evaluation research. Because the main intellectual roots of evaluation research are found there, social science concepts and research methods predominate. At the same time, the social sciences and natural sciences share the same basic approach to the observable world, so evaluation researchers play by the same rules of evidence as all scientists.

All social science fields have contributed to the development of evaluation research methods. It is not surprising, therefore, that the best evaluation research and the best evaluators draw on a number of disciplines, using an eclectic repertoire of concepts and methods. As we proceed, we will begin with the policy environment in which evaluation research is undertaken, because policy questions provide motivation for the entire evaluation research enterprise. Then, we move on to technical matters. However, the boundaries between policy concerns and technical concerns are often unclear, in part because they have implications for one another. From the start, we stress that evaluation research is not basic research.

Policy Space

The substantive roots of evaluation research rest in policy concerns, and evaluations are almost entirely confined to issues that are contained in the current "policy space." That is, evaluations are almost exclusively concerned with making judgments about policies and programs that are on the current agenda of policymakers (broadly construed to include a wide variety of "players," not just public officials). Clearly, the policy space is bound by time and space and does not encompass a permanently fixed set of policies and programs; it changes over time and it varies over political jurisdictions. For example, in the 1960s, concern about low-income households helped define a policy space in the United States that included direct income support, in the form of a "negative income tax," for households falling below the poverty line. In response, a number of evaluation projects explored what the impact of such support might be. In the 1980s, the national policy space no longer included a negative income tax. Rather, attention had shifted to "supply-side" economics, which holds that by stimulating economic growth for the nation as a whole, poor families would be helped as well. What followed were a number of evaluations of this "trickle-down" theory in which income distributions before and after the Reagan years were compared. By the mid 1990s, the policy space addressing poverty had shifted dramatically again. AFDC (Aid to Families with Dependent Children) came under stronger attack for promoting "dependency," and new programs to move welfare recipients into the labor force were fielded (Gans 1995; Handler 1995). A number of states conducted sophisticated evaluations of programs designed to promote the work effort of AFDC clients. Many of these evaluations were used to guide the reconstruction of public welfare under the Personal Responsibility and Work Obligation Reconciliation Act of 1996. In a similar fashion, in the mid 1970s, a serious drought across California led various communities in that state to consider a wide variety of water conservation programs. By the early 1980s, water conservation concerns dissipated, in part because the drought had passed. However, another drought stuck in the late 1980s, and water conservation programs again were front and center. By the early 1990s, drought conditions had passed, but economic and population growth in California was making water availability a chronic worry. Moreover, concerns about global climate change and its implications for precipitation were leading some observers to claim that water supplies for California might decline significantly over time (Gleick 1993). Water conservation was then taken to be but one tool with which to more generally "manage" the demand for water.

It is the almost exclusive attention to matters in current policy space that helps distinguish evaluation research from academic social science, and a good evaluation researcher knows how to determine what is in the policy space and what is not. For example, an academic social scientist might study the "urban underclass" as an intellectual matter and might in addition be genuinely concerned about their plight. In contrast, the evaluation researcher would focus on the current policy debates and especially social interventions that are being contemplated or are already in place. Still more concretely, the academic might have a long-standing interest in theories of segmented labor markets and undertake a study of the causes of teenage unemployment to test competing theories. The evaluator could certainly draw on insights from such research but might concentrate, for instance, on the impact of a particular job training program for unemployed teenagers.

Stakeholders

By virtue of its engagement in policy-space matters, evaluation research is saturated with political concerns. The outcome of an evaluation can be expected to attract the attention of persons, groups, and agencies who hold stakes in the outcome. These stakeholders (also sometimes called *interested parties*) include policymakers on executive and legislative levels; agencies and their officials who administer the policies or programs under scrutiny; the persons who deliver the services in question; often, groups representing the targets or beneficiaries of the programs, or the targets or beneficiaries themselves; and sometimes taxpayers and citizens in general. For almost all program issues, stakeholders may be in conflict, some favoring the program and some opposing it. And whatever the outcome of the evaluation may be, there are usually some who are pleased and some who are disappointed; it is usually impossible to please everyone. Thus, an evaluation showing that community policing does not reduce crime in a particular city (Kessler and Duncan 1996) might delight traditional law enforcement officers and anger reformers. Another example is an evaluation that ranks hospitals by the quality of medical care offered (Teasley 1996), which is bound to pit the highly rated hospitals against the others. In short, an evaluation report ordinarily is not regarded as a neutral document. Rather, it is scrutinized, often minutely, by stakeholders who are quick to discern how its contents affect their activities. Even when an evaluation is conducted in house by an agency concerned with its own activities, various stakeholders within the agency might appraise the report differently.

One implication is that evaluation research should not be undertaken by persons who prefer to avoid controversy or who have difficulty facing criticism. Often, moreover, the criticism is "political," more concerned with how the findings affect self-interest than with scientific quality. One illustration of late is the vitriolic attacks back and forth over virtually any evaluation of programs that restrict citizens' access to firearms or any evaluation of programs that expand citizens' access to firearms (Spitzer 1995). Another is the recent Fort Bragg evaluation showing that the provision of a full range of mental health services in a managed coordinated system, compared to fragmented and limited mental health services, did not lead to better mental health outcomes (Bickman et al. 1995). The evaluation was roundly attacked because managed mental health care had been strongly advocated by experts in the field. The general moral is that "for every evaluation finding there is equal and opposite criticism."

A second implication is that much greater care may need to be taken in the conduct of evaluation research than in the conduct of its academic cousin, basic research. Procedures bordering on the slipshod will surely come to the attention of critical stakeholders and render an evaluation report vulnerable. In addition, even for well-conducted studies, attacks will typically focus on "methodological issues" because, as noted earlier, *all* studies have methodological flaws (more on that shortly). Alleged methodological errors are easy targets, even when they could not materially affect the conclusions of the evaluation. For example, recording errors for a variable that was not even used in an evaluation may be highlighted to cast doubt on the rest of the data. Thus, an evaluation of the satisfaction that residents may have with how their public housing complex is managed (Van Ryzin 1996) may quite sensibly focus on the complex in which residents live as the unit of analysis. Yet if a few residents in a given complex are listed by error as living in the wrong apartment, the study may be easily subjected to ridicule.

A third implication is that the conduct of evaluation research often involves careful prior negotiations with stakeholders. For example, a key obstacle in evaluations of school-based "gang resistance education and training" (GREAT) is obtaining consent from principals, teachers, and especially from parents (Esbensen et al. 1996).

Program Effectiveness: Three Meanings

Although the importance of the political environment in which evaluation research is undertaken is difficult to overemphasize, political matters are hardly the whole story. A mixture of technical skills is the evaluator's ticket of admission, and in the end, it justifies his or her keep. We turn, then, to technical matters, beginning with conceptions of the proverbial bottom line: program effectiveness.

In the broadest sense, evaluations are concerned with whether or not programs or policies are achieving their goals. Discerning the goals of policies and programs is an essential part of an evaluation and almost always its starting point. However, goals are often stated vaguely and broadly, typically in an attempt to garner as much political support as possible. In that sense, many program designers are very much like politicians running for office, and in the words of more than one observer, "in order to succeed in politics, one must learn how to rise above one's principles."

Programs and policies that do not have clear and consistent goals cannot be evaluated for effectiveness. In response, a subspecialty of evaluation research, evaluability assessment, has developed to uncover the goals and purposes of policies and programs in order to judge whether or not they can be evaluated.

Insofar as goals are articulated, "effectiveness" is the extent to which a policy or program is achieving those goals. In practice, it cannot be overemphasized that the concept of effectiveness must always address the issue "compared with what?" For *marginal* effectiveness, the issue is dosage; the consequences of more or less of some intervention are assessed. For example, recently in California a strong local economy provided a tax windfall that the governor and legislature allocated in part for dramatic reductions in primary-school classroom size. The assumption was that with a better student–teacher ratio, student performance would improve. In this case, the "dose" was represented by the ratio of teachers to students, and the evaluation question was whether a greater "dose" of teacher contact would lead to better scores on standardized tests. The comparison was to performance before the student–teacher ratio was improved.

For *relative* effectiveness, the contrast is between a program and the absence of the program or between two or more program options. Note that the absence of a program is not nothing, but the status quo. For example, in a major turnaround in federal policy, a few government dams are being torn down to allow rivers to return to a more natural state. Among the potential benefits is restoration of former habitats for various species of salmon. The evaluation question is what impact this will have on salmon populations compared to their current numbers. It might turn out that the dramatic reductions in salmon observed over the past decade resulted from some other environmental stressor or from over-fishing (Rothschild 1996). Then no increases in salmon population might be observed. The key point, however, is that two different environmental interventions (dam and no dam) are being compared, one effectively the status quo and one an "innovation," even though technically it is an effort to restore part of the past.

Finally, it is common to consider effectiveness in dollar terms: *cost*-effectiveness. Comparisons are made in units of outcome per dollar. For example, finding and treating only individuals who have recently become infected with HIV would probably be less effective in slowing the AIDS pandemic than finding and testing all sexually active people. But it would be more cost-effective to concentrate on recently infected individuals because they may have already demonstrated some proclivity for high-risk sexual practices and because there is some evidence that the probability of transmission is highest in the first few months after infection (Pinkerton and Abramson 1996). That is, focusing on recently infected individuals would mean less cost per new case of AIDS prevented, because individuals most likely to pass the HIV along would be the targets.

Validity

It is one thing to properly conceptualize program effectiveness and quite another to determine empirically whether a program is effective. Determining effectiveness depends, in turn, on the validity of the evaluation. In other words, evaluation research shares with other research activities the overriding goal of achieving high validity. Little is learned from evaluations with low validity. Broadly stated, validity represents a set of scientific criteria by which the credibility of research may be judged. As such, it involves matters of degree; studies are more or less valid. For example, there is a heated controversy about the degree to which findings from studies using mice to determine the carcinogenic impact of various environmental pollutants may be properly applied to humans (Freedman and Zeisel 1988). Two issues are involved. First, there is the obvious concern about generalizing from mice to humans. A more subtle concern involves extrapolating from the doses given to mice to the exposure humans might experience. Because cancer is relatively rare in mice, the experimental mice are usually given enormous doses of potential carcinogens. That way, the researchers are more likely to have a sufficient number of mice with cancer to study. However, humans would not normally experience exposure at comparable levels. The critics argue, therefore, that chemical compounds, which at very high doses might cause cancer in mice, might not at low doses cause cancer in humans.

Evaluators may differ on which kinds of validity are most important (e.g., Cronbach 1982), and what *validity* means may change over time as methodological technology evolves. Nevertheless, it is common to emphasize four kinds of validity: construct validity, internal validity, external validity, and statistical conclusion validity (Cook and Campbell 1979). We will return to the four kinds of validity after laying a bit more groundwork.

In an ideal situation, policymakers are seeking a binary assessment about a social program: thumbs up or thumbs down. Either the program works or it does not. In addition, they are ideally seeking a specific number indicating how effective the program is. Thus, a prison vocational training program might reduce recidivism by 15%, or a nutrition program for pregnant women in low-income neighborhoods may increase the birth weight of infants by an average of 500 grams. A company's affirmative action program may increase by 15 the number of African Americans and Latinos hired.

As just noted, however, the world of program evaluation is never that simple. *All* assessments come with healthy amounts of uncertainty, and evaluation results necessarily have varying amounts of credibility. To be sure, studies with greater validity provide more credible results, but some uncertainty will always remain. That is, evaluation findings are not right or wrong, but more or less credible. Often, the uncertainty is expressed in how the role of chance is represented, but that is hardly the whole story.

It is perhaps important to stress that the uncertainty in evaluation results is effectively inherent in the social phenomena being studied, and no research methodology, even the ideal, can remove it. However, stronger research methods typically reduce the amount of uncertainty.

Measurement and Construct Validity

Measurement is nothing more than a systematic procedure to assign (real) numbers to objects. *Age,* for example, may be measured by the number of years between birth and the present. *Prior record* may be measured by a "1" if there is a previous conviction and a "0" if there is no previous conviction. *Attitudes toward water conservation* may be measured by a "3," "2," or "1," depending, respectively, on whether a person answers "agree," "uncertain," or "disagree" to a survey question on the importance of installing water-saving appliances. Measurement in evaluation research is sometimes discussed under the rubric of *construct validity* (Cook and Campbell 1979).

Better measures in general lead to better evaluations. A "good" measure is, in commonsense terms, one that is likely to measure accurately what it is supposed to measure. For example, a study that purports to evaluate whether firearms owned by "civilians" are effective for self-defense must at the very least determine how often firearms are used to thwart a potential crime. This has been attempted in several surveys, and it is now clear that unless the questionnaire is very carefully worded, enormously misleading findings can result. In particular, asking a respondent straight out whether he or she has used a firearm for self-defense can lead to gross overestimates. In one study, for instance (Kleck and Gertz 1995), there were more claims by respondents that guns were used to prevent a burglary than there were burglaries in which guns had been used to begin with (Cook et al. 1997; Hemenway 1997)! It would have been far better to first establish whether the respondent had an opportunity to use a gun for self-protection, obtain details on the nature of the incident, and then ask about the use of firearms. At the very least, a chronological approach seems to help respondents recall what actually transpired (Wentland and Smith 1993).

At a minimum, evaluation researchers should be aware of the critical distinction between two kinds of measurement error: *systematic* and *random*. When the measurement error is systematic, there will be on the average an overestimate or underestimate of the "true" attribute that is being measured. This is at the heart of the perennial controversy over whether standardized IQ tests properly tap "general intelligence" (Lord and Novick 1968). For instance, there could be two causes of systematic error in IQ tests. The tests may fail to capture certain kinds of cognitive abilities (e.g., creativity) or the tests may capture other attributes that are not part of cognitive ability (e.g., culture). In the first case, the test is underinclusive, whereas in the second case the test is overinclusive. Sometimes, the term *validity* is used when researchers consider whether a variable, such as an IQ test score, is measuring what it is supposed to measure (and only that).

When the measurement error is random (or "noise"), the measure, on the average, will equal the true value of the attribute, but will be inaccurate to varying degrees for individual instances. That is, the measured IQ for each person will be a flawed measure of intelligence, but if the IQ test could be given a large number of times to each person (with no learning effects), the average of each person's IQ scores would be equal to each person's true IQ. Sometimes the term *reliability* is used when researchers consider how much noise there is in a variable such as a person's IQ test score.

It should be clear that systematic measurement error can seriously distort one's evaluation findings. It is also true, however, that random measurement error can be very damaging. When the random measurement error is in the outcome variable(s) of interest, noise can obscure real treatment effects. That is, real results may be overlooked. For example, an evaluation of programs to teach college students about "safe sex" was complicated by the fact that it is sometimes difficult for people to accurately recall and report the details of sexual encounters (Berk, Abramson, and Okami 1995). As a result, it was hard to determine if sexual practices really changed at all, let alone in response to the education program.

When the random measurement error is in the treatment (e.g., who got which intervention) or the control variables (i.e., variables whose effects need to be disentangled from the effects of the treatment), estimates of the treatment effect can be systematically too high or too low. This may seem counterintuitive, but random error can in this instance lead to consistent underestimates or overestimates of the treatment impact. That is, estimates of treatment impact will be biased. Suppose in the safe-sex example that the treatment were measured by hours spent in the educational program. If the program is effective, students who spend more time in the program should engage in a greater number of safe-sex practices. But if the amount of time is measured with substantial noise, some of the students who appear to have spent a lot of time in the program in fact did not. So the observed relationship between time in the program and safe-sex practices would be a diluted version of the true relationship, and the impact of the program would be systematically underestimated.

What can be done? For systematic measurement error, there is but a single general strategy: Obtain one or more new measures that can be used to improve the flawed measures. For example, systematic measurement error in survey questions asking respondents about drunk driving arrests may be assessed by checking with local criminal justice records. From these and related studies, we know roughly by how much people tend to underreport in surveys socially undesirable behavior (Wentland and Smith 1993). From these studies, we also learn how better to ask about sensitive issues. For random measurement error, there are three related solutions. Under some circumstances, one can try to measure the same thing many different ways, and then use the average of the measures in any analysis. By using the average, the noise tends to cancel out. This approach is most common in standardized tests in which a number of questions that measure the same underlying skill may be included. In addition, this basic approach can be formally represented statistically, so that the information from multiple measures is directly built into the evaluation data analysis. Sometimes that may mean nothing more than directly correcting for attenuated effects (Lord and Novick 1968), such as those just described for classes teaching safe-sex practices to college students. But far fancier methods are also available in which the random measurement error is more explicitly represented (Everitt 1984; Fuller 1987). Finally, if the variable measured with random error is related to another variable that measured without random error, it is then possible in some situations to have the variable measured without error (or a function of it) partly "stand in" for the variable that has random error, even if the two variables are not really measuring the same thing. The substitute variable is often called an *instrumental variable* (Bowden and Turkington 1984).

Causality and Internal Validity

Many evaluation questions concern causal relations, such as whether or not a proposed program to ban diesel trucks from certain urban areas will "cause" reductions in air pollution. The literature on causality and causal inference is large and currently fraught with controversy (e.g., Angrist et al. 1996; Berk 1988b; Freedman 1991; Holland 1986; Holland and Rubin 1988; Pratt and Schlaifer 1984). Suffice it to say that by a *causal effect* we mean a comparison between the outcome had the intervention been introduced and the outcome had the intervention not been introduced. Thus, the causal effect of a ban on diesel trucks might be the concentration of aerosols had diesel trucks been banned compared to the concentration had the ban not been put in place. (Aerosols are particles that when lodged in the lungs are implicated in a number of chronic respiratory diseases.)

From the definition of a causal effect, it should be apparent that, in practice, causal effects cannot be directly observed. One cannot observe the concentration of aerosols simultaneously with and without the ban on diesel trucks in place. Rather, causal effects must be inferred. As a consequence, one might try to estimate the causal effect of the ban by comparing aerosol concentrations before the ban to concentrations after the ban. Or one might try to estimate the causal effect of the ban by comparing aerosol concentrations in an area with the ban in place to aerosol concentrations in an area without the ban.

In the first case, however, one must assume that no other changes had occurred that could affect aerosol concentrations in the interval between the earlier and later observational periods. In the second case, one must assume that the two areas are otherwise effectively identical on all factors that could influence aerosol concentrations. In short, the need to infer causal effects opens the door to inferential errors. In practice, therefore, whenever a causal relationship is proposed, alternative explanations must be addressed and, presumably, discarded. If such alternatives are not considered, one may be led to make "spurious" causal inferences; the causal relationship being proposed may not in fact exist. Sometimes this concern with spurious causation is addressed under the heading of *internal validity* (Cook and Campbell 1979). In our aerosol illustration, a before–after comparison may involve two different seasons. If the before period is in the summer and the after period is in the winter, observed differences in aerosol concentrations might result not from the ban on diesel trucks, but from changes in local weather conditions, such as the direction and strength of prevailing winds and the greater use of heating fuels in the winter.

Consideration of alternative causal explanations for the performance of programs is extremely important when plans to collect the data are formulated (Heckman and Robb 1985). For example, programs that deal with humans are all more or less subject to problems of self-selection (Heckman and Robb 1986); often persons who are most likely to be helped, or who are already on the road to recovery, are those most likely to participate in a program. Thus vocational training offered to unemployed adults is likely to attract those who would be most apt to improve their employment situation in any event. Or sometimes, program operators "skim off the cream" among target populations for participation in programs, thereby ensuring that such programs appear successful. In still other cases, events unconnected with the program produce changes that seem to result from the program being evaluated: An improvement in the speed with which cases are processed by a county's courts may seem to result from the addition of more prosecutors to the local district attorney's office, when actually the improvement may have been caused by an unconnected change in plea-bargaining practices.

We will have much more to say about causal inference later. But it is useful to briefly introduce here the gold standard for internal validity: *randomized experiments* (Boruch 1997), because, at least in principle, randomized experiments are the strongest tools available with which to infer cause.

The basic idea is that each member of a pool of research participants is assigned to the program or the comparison condition by random assignment, much as in a special kind of lottery. A chance mechanism is employed so that there is nothing about any participant that can be associated with the probability of being exposed to the program. The result is that, on the average, the program and comparison participants are comparable before the program is introduced and, therefore, average differences between the groups in outcome may be plausibly attributed to the program. Randomized experiments, if properly implemented, are the gold standard because alternative causal explanations for the findings are automatically ruled out; the chance mechanism guarantees within the bounds of the luck of the draw that all participants have the same probability of being exposed to the program. (See Rosenbaum 1995, chapter 2, for a technical discussion and more complex randomized experimental designs.) In this regard, randomized experiments are stronger than any other research design. The only major complication is that chance also has to be ruled out as an explanation. We will return to this issue several times in the pages ahead.

Randomized experiments are sometimes called *clinical trials* in biomedical research. The program being tested is a particular instance of a "treatment" or "intervention." Participants exposed to the treatment are usually called the *experimental group* or the *treatment group,* whereas participants exposed to the comparison are often called the *control group.* In practice, there can be several different treatments and, therefore, several different treatment groups, and the research participants are not limited to people. They may be any units: persons, households, classrooms, hospitals, neighborhoods, business enterprises, and so on. As we discuss later, however, random assignment is often impractical with larger units, such as neighborhoods, because of logistics and cost (Rossi 1998a).

Randomized experiments are very common in evaluation research (Berk et al. 1985), especially when concerns about internal validity are paramount. Numerous examples can be found in the fields of education, criminal justice, welfare, public health, tax administration, and job training (Boruch 1997). An interesting recent illustration is the set of randomized experiments conducted over the past decade on various forms of welfare reform. In those studies, welfare recipients are assigned to a variety of programs intended to encourage a transition from the welfare roles to gainful employment (Gueron and Pauly 1991). Perhaps the best-known instance is the GAIN (Greater Avenues for Independence) program in California, which seems to produce some small program benefits (Riccio et al. 1994).

Generalizability and External Validity

Whatever the empirical conclusions resulting from evaluation research, it is necessary to consider how broadly one can generalize the findings in question; that is, are the findings relevant to other times, other subjects, similar programs, and other program sites? Sometimes such concerns are raised under the rubric of "external validity" (Cook and Campbell 1979). It cannot be overemphasized that, if findings cannot be generalized, they are useless. Policymakers need to know how interventions of certain kinds work and whether those kinds of interventions are effective. Knowing how a particular program worked and how effective it was in itself has no value, because that program can never be exactly duplicated. The best that policymakers can do is mount a program that is (more or less) similar to the program evaluated.

Consider, for instance, a program to reduce the consumption of electricity during the middle of the day (the "peak-load" problem) by raising the price of electricity between 10:00 a.m. and 4:00 p.m. Such a program may be desirable because if the demand for energy is less "lumpy" (variable) over the course of the day, utility companies will be able to get by with less energy-producing capacity; there will be less need to have the capacity to supply energy at very high levels for a few hours each day.

Suppose the evaluation convincingly showed that raising the price by 15% led to a drop of 10% in electricity use during the peak-load hours. However, the economic environment in which the intervention was introduced is constantly changing, and this will affect not only the base price of electricity on which the 15% increase may be calculated but the fraction of each consumer's budget that is allocated to the purchase of electricity. For example, if the base price of electricity is low relative to the price of gas, consumers may be inclined to purchase electric stoves rather than gas stoves and electric clothes dryers rather than gas dryers. New homes may be built with electric heat rather than gas heat. Over the medium term, therefore, the consumption of electricity may *increase*. Moreover, consumer concern about energy shortages will depend on a variety of factors, such as the pricing policies of OPEC and how that is depicted in the American mass media. In short, it is far from obvious what use policymakers could make of the evaluation unless one grants some license to generalize.

The key, therefore, is being able to make statements about energy conservation programs *similar* to the one evaluated. If the study is well designed (more on that later) and if good social science theory exists on how consumers respond to price, policymakers may confidently conclude that, *in general*, peak-time price increases will reduce energy use during the middle of the day and that the response of consumers to increases in the price of electricity will be much like the responses estimated. For example, microeconomic theory may confirm that increases in the marginal (per unit) price will reduce consumption almost regardless of circumstances and that the price elasticity for particular commodities will be effectively constant across different times, places, and mixes of residential consumers. In other words, although the electricity conservation program evaluated is literally unique, it may well be possible to draw more general conclusions.

External validity, then, refers to the degree to which these kinds of generalizations are justified. More broadly, among the standard external validity concerns that can be raised about most evaluations is whether the findings are applicable to settings differing from the ones in which the evaluation was undertaken. *Settings* can include a country, state, county, city, neighborhood, school district, business firm, hospital, and so on. For example, "safe houses" for victims of spousal abuse may be effective only in large urban areas in which the location of the safe house can be kept secret. Likewise, an affirmative action program that might be effective in virtually all private universities might fail at public universities, in which the political constraints may be far more severe.

It is also common to wonder whether an evaluation's results would be applicable to persons who differ from the study's participants in abilities or in socioeconomic background. For example, the television program "Sesame Street" was found to be effective for preschool children from lower socioeconomic families but even more effective for children from middle-class families (Cook et al. 1975). In contrast, within California prisons, placing inmates in different custodial settings by a routinized "classification score" seems to effectively sort inmates by the risk of misconduct, regardless of whether the inmate is male or female (California Department of Corrections 1997). The same sorts of issues arise for all kinds of experimental units such as households, police departments, prisons, watersheds, and stands of trees.

There is also the problem of generalizing over time. For example, Maynard and Murnane (1979) found that transfer payments provided by the Gary Income Maintenance Experiment apparently increased the reading scores of children from the experimental families. One possible explanation is that, with income subsidies, parents (especially in single-parent families) were able to work less and, therefore, spend more time with their children. Even if this were true, it raises the question of whether similar effects would be found now, when inflation is taking a smaller bite out of the purchasing power of households.

Finally, there is the difficulty of generalizing over interventions, because no two treatments are likely to be identical. Consider, for instance, the program to deliver managed mental heath services in the Fort Bragg, North Carolina, catchment area (Bickman et al. 1995). Managed care in the military might be very different from managed care offered by the county department of children and family services, which in turn might be quite different from managed care delivered by a health care provider contracting with a Fortune 500 corporation. One cannot necessarily generalize from one intervention to another, because programs with the same name will often be different in content. For example, the range of mental health services offered may depend on who orchestrates the services: a primary care physician or clinical psychologist.

Another way of thinking about generalization is to recognize that programs vary in their robustness—that is, in their ability to produce the same results with different operators, with different clientele, in different settings, and at different historical times. Clearly, a robust program is highly desirable. For example, many medical interventions, such as vaccination programs for influenza, are relatively robust because, for purposes of fighting disease, medical treatments can often be effectively standardized, and humans tend to respond in a sufficiently homogeneous manner.

It should be clear that external validity is a vital issue in all evaluations, which may be handled well or poorly. Basically, there are three devices that evaluators can employ to improve external validity. First, an *unbiased sample* of a defined population (e.g., via a probability sample) justifies generalization back to that population (Kish 1965). Thus, findings from a random sample of students from a given high school may be generalized to all students in that school. However, the sampling procedures do *not* by themselves justify generalizations to students in other high schools, even in the same school district. In addition, the unbiased sample of students does not formally justify generalizing back to some population of interventions or time periods. We will have a lot more to say about such issues later.

Moreover, one must be careful to distinguish between how a sample is designed and how it is implemented. In this regard, a key concept is the *response rate* (sometimes also called the *cooperation rate*), roughly defined as the number of units in the final sample divided by the total number of units that should have been in the sample as designed. Response rates substantially less than 100% can produce very misleading results if the "missing" units differ in important ways from the units included. For example, in the research on school-based gang prevention programs cited earlier (Esbensen et al. 1996), many parents did not give permission for their children to participate, and there was reason to worry that the children of noncooperating parents were more likely to be the very children at greater risk for gang involvement.

Second, *replications* of a given evaluation may be used to incrementally define the boundaries within which generalization is possible. By replications we mean new studies that are as similar as possible to the original study for which generalization was problematic. Note that it is the study that is being replicated; the original findings may or may not be replicated. For example, a randomized experiment in Minneapolis showing that arresting wife batterers reduced their subsequent violent behavior was replicated in six different cities (Berk et al. 1992). The goal, in part, was to determine the range of settings in which arresting wife batterers is truly a deterrent. The content of an arrest, for instance, varied by jurisdiction, with arrests in some areas including a day or more in jail (awaiting a bail hearing) and arrests in other areas leading to almost immediate release after booking. Although the results of the replications remain controversial, it is fair to say that the earlier Minneapolis findings were not fully reproduced. Generalizing the Minneapolis results is very risky, therefore.

Third, *existing theory* or *empirical generalizations* may be used for generalizing evaluation findings. For example, microeconomic theory asserts that virtually all consumers will respond to price increases by buying less of the particular commodity. Hence, an evaluation in a single community showing that increasing the price of water leads to reduced residential water use may be widely generalized (Berk et al. 1981). Unfortunately, it is very rare in the social sciences to find a theory that both is widely accepted and leads to broad generalizations.

Chance and Statistical Conclusion Validity

The nature of chance in social phenomena has a long and controversial history, but for present purposes, chance plays a role whenever uncertainty exists. Basically, there are three (probably complementary) perspectives. First, uncertainty may result from how the data were collected. Second, uncertainty may derive from our ignorance about particular social or physical phenomena. Third, uncertainty may be an inherent part of all social or physical phenomena. Each of these perspectives on the role of chance will be considered later. Regardless of which of the three perspectives one favors, it is always important that the role of chance be properly taken into account. When formal, quantitative findings are considered, this is sometimes addressed under the heading of *statistical conclusion validity* (Cook and Campbell 1979), and the problem is whether "statistical inference" has been taken into account properly.

Thus, just as flipping four heads in a row does not necessarily mean that a coin is biased (because a fair coin will produce four heads in a row once in a while), finding that students exposed to a driver's education course have fewer accidents than those who were not does not necessarily mean that the program was a success. The difference in the number of accidents between students who took a driver's education class and students who did not may have been produced by a chance mechanism analogous to flipping a coin. Unless the role of such chance factors is assessed formally, it is impossible to determine if the program effects are real or illusory.

Similar issues concerning the operation of chance appear in non-quantitative work as well, although formal assessments of the role of chance are difficult to undertake in such studies. Nevertheless, it is important to ask whether the reported findings rest on observed behavioral patterns that occurred with sufficient frequency and stability to warrant the conclusions that they are not *simply* the result of chance. Good ethnographers often address the role of chance by collecting a lot of data, which allows an assessment of whether certain observed phenomena occur so often in particular ways that "the luck of the draw" can implicitly be ruled out.

Having provided a brief taste of the issues, we can return to the three perspectives on chance. Consider first how evaluation data may be collected. Sampling error can occur whenever one is trying to make statements about some population of interest from observations gathered on a subset of that population. For example, one might be studying a sample of students from among those attending a particular school, a sample of teachers from the population of teachers in a particular school system, or even a sample of schools from a population of schools within a city, county, or state. Yet, although it is typically more economical to work with samples, the process of sampling necessarily introduces the prospect that any conclusions based on the sample may differ from conclusions that might have been reached had the full population been studied instead. Indeed, one can well imagine obtaining different results from different subsets of the population. Although any subset that is selected from a larger population for study purposes may be called a *sample*, some subsets may be worse than having no observations at all.

The act of sampling must be accomplished according to rational selection procedures that guard against the introduction of selection bias. A biased sample is one in which the statistics calculated will on the average (over many samples) underestimate or overestimate the properties of the population in question (e.g., mean household income in the United States). An unbiased sample is one in which the statistics calculated will on the average not underestimate or overestimate the properties of the population in question.

A class of such sampling procedures that yield unbiased samples are called *probability samples* in which every element in a population has a known, nonzero chance of being selected. Probability samples are difficult to execute and are often quite expensive, especially when dealing with populations that are hard to locate. Yet there are such clear advantages to such samples, as opposed to haphazard and potentially biased methods of selecting subjects, that probability samples are almost always to be preferred over less rational methods. (See Kish 1965 for a classic treatment of sampling; Levy and Lemeshow 1991 for a very accessible exposition; Sarndal, Swensson, and Wretman 1992 for an advanced approach emphasizing the link between modeling and sampling; and Sudman 1976 for some practical sampling strategies.)

Fortunately, when samples are drawn with probability procedures, disparities between statistics calculated from a sample and the respective population values can result only from the luck of the draw. So, with the proper use of statistical inference, one can place confidence intervals around estimates from probability samples, or ask whether a sample estimate differs in a statistically significant manner from an assumed population value. In the case of confidence intervals, one can obtain an assessment of how much "wiggle" there is likely to be in one's sample estimates. In the case of significance tests, one can reach a decision about whether a sample statistic (e.g., a mean SAT score) differs from some assumed value in the population (e.g., 600). For example, insofar as the mean SAT score from a random sample of students differs from some national norm, one can determine if the disparity represents a statistically significant difference—that is, a difference large enough that the score could not have occurred easily by chance alone.

A second kind of chance factor associated with data collection stems from the process by which experiment participants may be "assigned" to experimental and control groups. For example, it may turn out in an educational evaluation that the assignment process yields an experimental group that, on the average, contains brighter students than the control group. This may confound any genuine treatment effects with preexisting differences between experimentals and controls; here, the impact of some positive treatment such as self-paced instruction will be artificially enhanced because the experimentals were already performing better than the controls.

Much as in the case of random sampling, for experiments in which the assignment to treatment group or control group is undertaken with probability procedures, the role of chance can be taken into account. In particular, it is possible to determine whether the outcome differences between experimentals and controls are statistically significant. If the disparities are statistically significant, chance (through the assignment process) is eliminated as an explanation, and the evaluator can then begin making substantive sense of the results. It is also possible to place confidence intervals around estimates of the treatment effect(s) indicating roughly the likely range of the effects, given that any estimate is subject to random variation.

To summarize, it often makes very good research sense to introduce chance processes into data collection procedures. Random sampling is an excellent way to help ensure the quality of one's sample drawn from a population, and random assignment is an excellent way to help ensure the quality of comparisons between experimental and control groups. But the price of both procedures (typically small compared to the price of not using chance procedures) is that one must calibrate the impact of chance.

Chance may enter one's data independent of how the data were collected. It surfaces even if the total population of interest is studied and no assignment process or sampling procedure is undertaken. Under one conception, chance is introduced by measurement. We raised this prospect earlier when we discussed random measurement error and reliability. That is, the uncertainty derives from the measurement process itself. In the context of our current discussion, one can usefully think of measurement as a social process in which human activities of various sorts "cause" numbers to be attached to objects. Indeed, one can formulate a causal model of measurement that includes a "noise" component. Thus, obtaining a figure from coroner's reports of the number of homicides in a particular city depends on the social processes by which certain deaths are labeled as homicides, rather than accidents or suicides. Often facts are ambiguous, so the determinations of the "cause of death" involve a lot of guesswork.

Under a second conception, chance variation is introduced through the impact of a large number of real-world factors, sometimes called *perturbations* or *errors*, about which the researcher is at least partially uninformed. For example, a student's performance on a standardized test may be explained in part by his or her cognitive abilities. In addition, the performance may be affected by how much sleep he or she had the night before, anxiety levels, distractions during the test, whether he or she ate a proper breakfast, a recent quarrel with a sibling, and a host of other factors. Only the first may be understood and measured. The aggregate effect of the rest is the impact of chance. In principle, therefore, the world is deterministic; chance is an artifact of our ignorance. In practice, however, given that at least partial ignorance is a fact of life, the social phenomena are treated as if they contain a significant chance component.

Under a third conception, chance may be an inherent property of social life (and the physical world in general). The mechanisms involved are well beyond the scope of this book (see, for example, Briggs and Peat 1989), but the basic idea is that social life may be in part like the break in a game of eight ball. The curvature of the balls means that very small and seemingly insignificant displacements in which two balls make contact lead to large differences in the angles at which the balls separate. That is, very small initial differences produce very large consequences. And just as where the balls will stop after the break has a very large element of uncertainty, so does social life. For example, the difference of just a few points on the LSATs can determine a student's chances of getting into a particular law school. That outcome, in turn, can have important long-term career implications. Likewise, television shows can live or die by a very few rating points.

Sometimes it is hard to ascertain whether any of these conceptions of chance are relevant for a particular evaluation. A good test is to ask the following question: "If it were possible to go back to the beginning and repeat the study from scratch, would the results turn out the same?" If the answer is effectively yes, chance plays no role in the evaluation. If the answer is effectively no, chance plays at least some role, and then it is critical to think through the sources and meaning of the uncertainty. For example, in a determination of whether African Americans are underrepresented in a particular business firm, a head count based on personnel records would yield a number that should be reproduced if the count were undertaken again. Thus, the number itself effectively contains no uncertainty. In contrast, if the head count were made by observing and recording the apparent race of employees as they reported for work on a given day, it is clear that were the head count repeated, the result could well be different. At the very least, day to day variation in absentees could affect the outcome.

Under any of the three conceptions of chance, one can sometimes proceed in practice with the assumption that, whatever the program processes at work, also at work will be other forces that have some impact on outcomes of interest. These forces typically are treated as if they were a large number of small perturbations that on the average cancel one another. Then it is a small step to abstractly conceptualize these perturbations as a formal chance component behaving as if it were a variable drawn at random from some known distribution that has a mean of zero and some variance. Thinking back to the test-taking example discussed previously, each neglected factor (e.g., amount of sleep the night before, what the student ate for breakfast the morning of the test, and so forth) introduces small amounts of variation in a child's performance. For any given day, therefore, the small neglected factors may be treated in the aggregate as a random draw from a population of test-taking "perturbations." This distribution, in turn, has a mean of zero and some spread. Thus, there will be chance variation in performance that needs to be taken into account. Then, as before, one can apply tests for statistical significance or confidence intervals. One can still ask, for example, if some observed difference between experimentals and controls is larger than might be expected from chance factors or estimate the wiggle in experimental–control disparities.

However, it is critical to stress that to proceed in this manner, one must make assumptions about the social processes that generated the data that may or may not make a lot of sense. In this instance, does it make sense to assume that the many small factors affecting test performance are unrelated? For example, can one assume that a lack of sleep the night before and failing to then eat an adequate breakfast are unrelated? (Not if the child is ill.) Can one assume that the chance factor operating on one day is unrelated to the chance factor operating the next? (Again, not if the child is ill.) And if either kind of dependence exists, the usual statistical assumptions necessary for statistical inference may not apply. In short, the automatic application of conventional statistical inference to data that are not generated by chance procedures designed and implemented by the researcher can lead one into a "science fiction model" of statistical inference (Berk and Freedman 1995). The best antidote is a solid understanding of the social processes that generated the uncertainty and a careful mapping of this understanding to an appropriate statistical model. Suffice it to say, this typically is very difficult to do.

In short, statistical conclusion validity speaks to the quality of inferential methods applied and not to whether some result is statistically significant. Statistical conclusion validity may be high or low independent of judgments about statistical significance. (For a more thorough discussion of these and other issues of statistical inference in evaluation research, and statistical inference more generally, see Barnett 1982; Berk and Brewer 1978; Berk et al. 1995; and Leamer 1978. For a truly outstanding introductory text, see Freedman, Pisani, and Purves 1997.)

The Role of Theory

It seems obvious that evaluation research could usefully exploit "theory" related to the social problem being addressed and how the programmatic response should operate. Theory could be used to help develop programs, formulate evaluation designs, guide the data collection, and inform the analysis of those data. That is, theory would have many of the benefits it has in science more generally. Some have called this *theory-driven evaluation* (Chen 1990; Chen and Rossi 1980) or *theory-based evaluation* (Weiss 1997).

So far, however, theory has not lived up to its promise in evaluation research. To begin, there is no agreement on what constitutes theory. For some evaluation researchers, a mere typology qualifies. For example, although it may be important to distinguish the urban underclass from the working poor, those two categories by themselves do not address cause-and-effect relationships. For other evaluation researchers, any set of statements that link causes to effects qualifies. It does not matter how precise the statements are, whether they are internally consistent, whether they can be examined with data, or whether they are consistent with past empirical work and past theory supported by research. An instructive example is the statement that the death penalty deters homicides. Note that unless one also knows what the alternative to the death penalty is (e.g., life imprisonment), the statement is effectively meaningless. The "compared to what?" aspect is completely ignored.

Fortunately, there are some evaluation researchers for whom the theory to be used must meet the same standards as theory in science (or at least social science). Perhaps the most common examples are found in microeconomics and may explain in part the very important role that economists have played in evaluation research. Examples from sociology, political science, and psychology are more difficult to find.

When the so-called theory is really just a typology, or when it is poorly formulated, very little is brought to the table. It should not be surprising, therefore, if the "theory" proves to be useless. The problem for good theory is that there may be very little that addresses the problems at hand. Perhaps the greatest success has come in the use of theory from microeconomics when understanding of the social problem or program can be enhanced with insights about how markets function or how individuals act to maximize utility. Good examples can be found in the long history of attempts to address poverty in America. The most optimistic summary is that the use of theory in evaluation research is currently hampered by a scarcity of good theory. With better theory will come greater benefits for evaluation research. Unfortunately, if the past is any indication, dramatic improvements in social science theory are not likely to come quickly.

Putting It All Together in a Research Design

To briefly summarize our discussion so far, planning an evaluation requires a number of decisions that will affect the validity of the research. First, choices have to be made about how the observed units (e.g., people, neighborhoods, schools) will be selected. Probability sampling is one example. Second, decisions have to be made about how measurement will be undertaken. For example, an arrest might be measured by an arrest report filed by a police officer. Third, it is also essential to consider how the treatment may be delivered. Random assignment is one instance. Plans for undertaking these three activities—

selecting the units, measuring, and delivering the intervention—constitute the research design of an evaluation.

Although the research design speaks to the validity of the study, there are other planning decisions that affect the relevance of the evaluation and whether the research design can be effectively implemented. In the case of relevance, the intervention must approximate as closely as possible the options in the policy space. In addition, the outcome measures must reflect an outcome that policymakers care about. If the goal of a program is to reduce crime, for example, reducing arrests may or may not be a reasonable proxy (given that many crimes are not reported and that arrests are made for only a fraction of reported crimes). In the worst of all possible worlds, a demonstrable program effect is dismissed because it is the wrong program and the wrong outcome.

In the case of implementation, the research design must be translated into a set of concrete activities that may be undertaken with the resources, personnel, and time available. This is often difficult. For example, it may be impossible to obtain access to police arrest reports needed to measure criminal activity. Parents may prohibit their children from participating in an experimental sex education class at school. Or overweight individuals may not adhere to the low-calorie diet that was part of the health experiment for which they initially volunteered. We will have more to say about such practical issues later.

The Best Possible Strategy

In the next chapters, the general issues just raised will be addressed in more depth. Before proceeding, however, it is important to stress that practical constraints may intervene in the "real world" of evaluation research, even when an ideal marriage is made between the evaluation questions posed and the empirical techniques employed. Problems of cost, timeliness, political feasibility, and other difficulties may prevent the ideal from being realized. This in turn will require the development of a "second-best" evaluation package (or even third-best), more attuned to what is possible in practice. Yet, practical constraints do not *in any way* justify a dismissal of technical concerns; if anything, technical concerns become even more salient when less desirable evaluation procedures are employed.

3

Designing and Testing New Programs

A Chronological Perspective

The Basic Questions

Virtually all evaluation research begins with one or more policy questions in search of answers. Such questions may include how widespread a social problem is, whether any program can be enacted that will ameliorate a problem, whether an existing program is effective, whether an existing program is producing enough benefits to justify its cost, and so on. The following chronological sequence is implied:

1. identification of policy issues,
2. formulation of policy responses
3. design of programs,
4. improvement of programs,
5. assessment of program functioning and impact, and
6. determination of cost-effectiveness.

In practice, sometimes not all six activities are addressed, often with good reason. For example, an evaluation of an ongoing social program such as Social Security might properly begin with the fourth issue, *improvement of programs.* Less frequently, the questions are addressed in another chronological order. For example, a decision might be made on political grounds to change the Social Security system. Then the precise nature of those changes would have to be delineated after an empirical analysis of whose needs are not being properly met. However, the six activities provide an initial conceptual framework for what lies ahead.

Fitting the Evaluation Strategy to the Problem

Each of the questions raised by a particular evaluation may be tackled at levels varying in intensity and thoroughness. When great precision is needed and ample resources are available, the most powerful evaluation procedures may be employed. When the occasion demands approximate answers or when resources are in short supply, "rough-and-ready" (and usually speedier) procedures can be used. Correspondingly, the answers supplied vary in quality; the findings of some evaluations are more credible than others, but all genuine evaluations produce findings that are better than speculation. They are also likely to produce better findings than conventional wisdom, especially if the wisdom is ideologically congenial. For example, it is believed by many that the death penalty deters would-be murderers despite study after study failing to find any deterrent effects.

This does not mean that evaluators can use any means available. Rather, they should use the best possible procedures, given available resources and constraints. This means more than lip service. It is all too common to hear in response to criticism of a slipshod evaluation the very lame excuse that "it was the best we could do under the circumstances," when, in fact, technically superior (and often less wasteful) procedures easily could have been applied.

Given the diversity of policy questions to be answered and enormous variations in available resources, it should not be surprising that there is no single "best way" to proceed. Evaluation research must draw on a variety of perspectives and on a pool of heterogeneous procedures. Thus, approaches that might be useful for determining what activities were actually undertaken under some educational program, for instance, might not be appropriate when the time comes to determine whether the program was worth the money spent. In a similar way, techniques that may be effective in documenting how a program is functioning on a day-to-day basis may prove inadequate for the task of assessing the program's ultimate impact.

The choice among evaluation methods depends in the first place on the particular question posed; appropriate evaluation techniques must be explicitly linked to each distinct policy question. Although this point may seem simple enough, it has been overlooked far too often, resulting in a forced fit between an evaluator's preferred method and particular questions at hand.

Another result is an evaluation research literature padded with empty, sectarian debates between warring camps of "true believers." For example, there has been a long and somewhat tedious controversy about whether assessments of the impact of social programs are best undertaken with research designs in which research participants are randomly assigned to experimental and control groups or through theoretically derived causal models of how the program works. In fact, the two approaches are complementary and can be wedded effectively (Angrist et al. 1996; Heckman and Robb 1985; Rossi, Berk, and Lenihan 1980).

In the second place, the choice among evaluation methods is conditioned by the resources available and by the amount of precision needed. For example, independent of available resources, a sample of elderly individuals as small as 300 may be sufficient to establish that a significant number of senior citizens have incomes below the poverty line. That is, the sample is large enough to document the existence of a social problem. However, if the program design requires a precise estimate of how many such individuals there are, a sample of several thousand (or larger) may be needed.

Likewise, it is important to consider the ratio of program costs to evaluation costs. Devoting more resources to an evaluation than to the program being evaluated is probably overkill or political suicide, unless there are larger issues at stake. For example, a particular program may be an exemplar standing in for a number of other, related programs. The rationale may be that if the exemplar shows no beneficial effects, such effects are unlikely from its garden-variety cousins. Under these circumstances, a substantial investment in the evaluation may be a very good idea.

Nor does it make sense to plan an evaluation that will take several years to complete when the answers it will supply are needed within

a few weeks. The information will arrive too late to be useful.
Moreover, evaluators can sometimes be duped into undertaking an
evaluation where the stakeholders' goal is to delay an important policy
decision. That is, there is no real interest in the evaluation results.
There is only an interest in slowing the political process. This is
particularly common in calls for "more research" on environmental
interventions. Local environmental groups, for instance, may call for
more research on risks to endangered species to stop the development
of a housing subdivision, or a major oil refinery will call for more
research on air quality and respiratory diseases to stop the imposition
of pollution controls.

Finally, evaluations need to be tailored to the degree of importance
of the issue under scrutiny. At one extreme, routine issues for potentially low-impact programs probably do not deserve to be evaluated
with any degree of care. To borrow from wisdom attributed to John
Tukey, "If it is not worth doing, it is not worth doing well." For
example, it may make very little substantive difference whether cloth
diapers are superior (or inferior) to disposable diapers. Hence, it is
not worthwhile investing many (if any) resources in evaluating their
comparative merits. Yet, such judgments often are not straightforward.
Although the two kinds of diapers may perform similarly with respect
to hygiene, they may have very different environmental consequences.
Cloth diapers need to be washed, which means the application of
detergents and energy to heat water. Disposable diapers wind up in
landfills where they degrade very slowly. And, of course, the issue
might be extremely salient to diaper manufacturers.

In contrast, policies dealing with central issues and programs that
are very expensive usually deserve the most careful evaluation possible. Recall our earlier discussions of the role of greenhouse gases in
global warming. Clearly, the issues are complex, highly political, and
probably monumental in their consequences. Thus, it would be foolish
to settle for anything less than the very best. The same case can be
made for all of the enacted recent reforms of the welfare system in the
United States and current proposals to replace the national income tax
with a flat tax, a sales tax, or a value-added tax.

The Policy Contexts of Evaluation

The six chronological activities listed can be placed in a richer and
broader framework of two evaluation contexts. *Policy and program*

formulation is the first, in which questions are raised about the nature and amount of some identified problem, whether appropriate policy actions can be taken, and whether programs that may be proposed are appropriate and effective. In other words, the first context looks to the *future* and what *might* be done. *Examinations of existing policies and programs* is the second, in which attention is directed toward whether extant policies are appropriate and whether current programs have had their intended effects. Thus, the second context reviews the *past* to *inform the future*.

Although these two broad contexts, like the earlier six activities, may be regarded as sequential, it often happens that the unfolding policy process may bypass earlier steps. Many major programs have truncated policy formation stages, going straight from the drawing boards of executive agencies or legislatures to full-scale operation. A recent example is the international controls on CFCs, the compounds that destroy stratospheric ozone above geographic poles. Once the meteorology and atmospheric chemistry were reasonably well understood, international accords in 1987, 1990, and 1993 rapidly led to programs to reduce CFC emissions. After the basic research was in, the necessary programs were "obvious"; there was no apparent need to field-test the programs. Evaluations since suggest that the programs have been moderately successful (de Gruijl 1995). The Head Start and school lunch programs also were launched with little program testing beforehand (Ziegler and Muenchow 1992). In these cases, however, there was no compelling basic research to justify the program, and whether Head Start was truly effective was not seriously questioned until some years after the program had been in place. Alternatively, many programs never get beyond the testing stage, because of demonstrated ineffectiveness, political opposition (e.g., contract learning: Gramlich and Koshel 1975), or changes in the policy space (e.g., the negative income tax proposals: Rossi and Lyall 1974).

Looking to the Future: Some Steps in Policy and Program Formulation

Some Background

Proposals for policy changes and new programs presumably arise out of dissatisfaction with the status quo. Sometimes, existing policies and programs are not performing as hoped or the problem they were designed to address has changed (or was misread). For example, hardly a week goes by without visible dissatisfaction being expressed about the ways public policy and programs are responding to the "drug problem" (Bertram et al. 1996; Riley 1995). Sometimes, new problems arise that were previously unaddressed. For example, current congressional concern about global warming is effectively new, although scientists have been studying the problem for decades. Ideally, scientific information may be brought to bear on both the nature of the social problem and the potential programmatic responses.

It is important that the previous paragraph not be misunderstood. In particular, we are not implying that the solutions offered by policymakers will necessarily confront the "real" problem in some objective sense. The "real" problem may be far from obvious, and certain responses may be immediately seen as impractical or politically unpalatable. For example, is the "real" problem with narcotics the large number of people who are addicted *or* the current policy that criminalizes the use of narcotics? Some argue that criminalization leads to a variety of problems, such as crimes committed to support the purchase of drugs and homicides caused by inner-city gangs fighting to control the drug trade in their neighborhoods. Yet, even if the second definition is preferred, for a policymaker to support decriminalization is at this time to commit political suicide. Put another way, defining a "social problem" is ultimately a political process, the outcome of which does not simply flow from an assessment of available information. Thus, although it would be hard to argue against providing the best possible data on potential areas of need, there is no necessary correspondence between patterns in those data and what eventually surfaces as a subject of concern. To overstate the case just a bit, never attribute to stupidity what can be explained by politics.

For example, in an analysis of pending legislation designed to reduce adolescent pregnancy, the General Accounting Office (GAO 1986) found that none of the legislation addressed teenage fathers. Every proposal treated adolescent pregnancy as if teenage girls conceive alone. Likewise, concerns about water shortages following the dry summer of 1988 typically failed to address the real possibility that water has been priced far too cheaply. The social problem definition did not acknowledge that too much water was used inefficiently, but rather assumed that the supply of water was inadequate. (See also Berk and Rossi 1976 for a more thorough discussion of problem-definition issues.)

An extremely controversial illustration that underscores the political nature of social problem definition is the famous census undercount. Although the cooperation rates for the U.S. census are very high overall, the cooperation rates for minorities in urban areas are lower. As a result, the populations for urban areas with large numbers of minorities are undercounted, which among other things affects the distribution of congressional seats and the dispersal of federal funds. A number of proposals have been made to obtain better counts of urban minorities, but they have their own set of problems (Freedman and Wachter 1996). For Democrats in Congress, the social problem is underrepresentation of ethnic groups and recent immigrants, who are likely to favor democratic candidates. Also, Democratic representatives are more likely to represent such areas to begin with. Republicans in Congress generally oppose efforts to alter how the census collects its data from urban areas. Although the undercount is acknowledged to be real enough, in their view its small size does not justify altering a data collection system that overall is doing an excellent job. That is, the social problem is not serious enough to try to fix, especially when it is not clear that the proposed solutions will actually provide more complete and accurate data.

Some final qualifications: In principle and in practice, there is no useful distinction between the formation of new policies and programs and the improvement of existing policies and programs. A proposed improvement is nothing but a proposed change. Correspondingly, evaluation procedures applicable to entirely new policies and programs are suitable for proposed changes in existing policies and programs. Therefore, the discussion that follows does not distinguish between them.

Stage 1: Defining the Problem

A social problem is a social construction. That is, a condition defined as problematic becomes a problem. Moreover, the particular manner in which the social problems are articulated may have dramatic effects on the kinds of remedies that are suggested. For example, two contending legislative proposals may each address the needs of homeless persons, one identifying the homeless as low-income individuals who have no kin on whom to be dependent, and the other defining homelessness as the lack of access to conventional shelter. The first definition centers attention on social isolation, and the second concentrates on the availability of affordable housing. It is likely that the ameliorative actions that follow will be different as well. The first might emphasize a program to reconcile estranged individuals with their relatives, and the second might imply a subsidized housing program (Rossi 1989).

To pursue another example, the presence of hazardous substances in storm drains may be defined either as an exposure problem or as a production problem. In the first instance, appropriate programs might emphasize how best to educate swimmers to avoid contaminated areas into which the storm drains empty. The second definition might lead to surveillance of potential polluters and sanctions for violating local pollution ordinances (Duke and Breswick 1997). Note that these two definitions are not contradictory; rather, each highlights an aspect of the problem.

The defining of social problems is, of course, not a task for which evaluators are uniquely trained. Lawyers, judges, staff in administrative agencies, and substantive specialists of various kinds (e.g., hydrologists in the case of water supply) are also trained in how to think about social problems. In addition, there is often a large number of "lay experts" who are sometimes more sophisticated than the credentialed experts. Too many credentialed experts seem to know absolutely everything about positively nothing.

There is a special role that evaluators can play in this portion of the evaluation process; they can help all parties think through the substantive and methodological implications of alternative social problem definitions. For example, it is clear that the two definitions of storm drain pollution given previously focus on slightly different (albeit overlapping) phenomena, but they also contain clues about the underlying causal factors. Moreover, whereas the first definition leads to a widespread educational effort for the population at large, the second suggests narrowly focused oversight efforts directed at business firms and municipalities. The former may be more expensive, but also more palatable politically. Yet, it might be easier to monitor the more focused intervention and estimate program impact, perhaps because data are already routinely collected on storm drain discharges. In short, judgments about definitional issues often require substantive and methodological knowledge that evaluators often have (or can easily get).

The evaluator can also play an important role by raising for discussion the fit between popular conceptions of the problem and the implicit or explicit definitions included in the legislative or administrative remedies. In this connection, the evaluator would ordinarily refer to legislative proceedings, including committee hearings and floor debates, opinion journals, newspaper and magazine editorials, and other sources in which discussions of the problem may appear. This "homework" can be used to provide policymakers with a wide range of social-problem formulations before a final conception is accepted. Otherwise, one risks an irrelevant evaluation. Moreover, as the problem definition is being constructed, it is vital for evaluators to make explicit what is going on; important options otherwise may be foreclosed. Policymakers should be constantly reminded that there are opportunity costs to their decisions. Otherwise, one risks having policymakers later dissociate themselves from the evaluation, claiming that they were misunderstood or misled when the evaluation was designed.

Evaluators can also be useful in working backward with policymakers from the proposed policies and program to the implied problem definitions. For example, a birth control education program for unwed teenagers may be implicitly defining the problem of teenage pregnancies in terms of illegitimate births. However, this formulation ignores the large number of births to married teenagers. Likewise, an affirmative action program for graduate training in the natural sciences may incorrectly assume that the pool of minority undergraduates properly prepared for graduate work in the natural sciences is as large as the comparable pool of White undergraduates.

Finally, for certain kinds of social problems, their very definition (as opposed to their size and scope, which we address later) may require surveying interested groups or the general population. For example, a routine question on public opinion polls that has been asked for two generations is, "What are the most important problems facing the country today?" Although this is not a very sophisticated way to approach social-problem definition, it is nevertheless regularly used by politicians to target their public appeals. More sophisticated examples focus on specific substantive areas and ask respondents who help articulate the dimensions of the problem. For example, Berk and Schulman (1995a) gave respondents a set of possible future climate scenarios in order to determine what facets of climate change they defined as most problematic. Such information is important because unless the public definition is taken into account, public support for various policy responses might not be forthcoming. In short, there can be a very direct role for an evaluator in problem definition when survey methods are desirable.

Stage 2: Where Is the Problem and How Big Is It? Needs Assessments

Proper design of a public program and projection of its costs require good information on the density, distribution, and overall size of the problem in question. For example, in providing financial support for emergency shelters for homeless persons in the United States, it would make a very significant difference if the total homeless population is approximately 3.5 million or approximately 350,000 (both estimates have been advanced). It would also make a big difference whether the problem was located primarily in central cities or whether it can be found in equal densities in small and large places (Koegel, Burnam, and Morton 1996; Rossi 1989).

An identified problem often is a complex mix of related conditions; planning requires information on that complexity. Returning to the example of homelessness, the proportions of the homeless suffering from chronic mental illness, chronic alcoholism, or physical disabilities need to be known in order to design an appropriate mix of interventions.

It is much easier to identify and define a problem than to develop valid estimates of its density and distribution. For example, consider the issue of hate crimes. According to recent statutes, *hate crimes* are defined as person or property offenses in which the race, ethnicity, nationality, religion, or sexual orientation of the victim figures significantly in the offender's motives. Hate crimes are routine material for the evening news, and they are universally condemned. However, obtaining reliable information on the numbers and kinds of hate crimes has been nearly impossible (Berk 1990). One problem is that much of the available data comes from "hot lines" organized by advocacy groups where coverage is highly suspect. Another problem is that the line between hate crimes and other crimes is often unclear and vulnerable to varying interpretations. Thus, there are often differences between individual police officers and between police officers and investigating detectives on whether a particular incident is a hate crime (Boyd, Hamner, and Berk 1996). Finally, like all crimes, only reported hate crimes can become part of the official record.

Through their knowledge of the existing literature (consisting of government reports, published and unpublished studies, and limited-distribution reports) and their understanding of which designs and methods lead to credible results, evaluation researchers are in a good position to collate and assess whatever information exists on the issues in question. Equal emphasis is given in the last sentence to "collate" and "assess"; unevaluated information can often be as bad as no information at all.

For some issues, existing data sources may be of sufficient quality to be used with confidence. For example, information that is routinely collected by either the Current Population Survey or the decennial census is likely to be of adequate quality. Likewise, data available in many of the statistical series routinely collected by federal agencies are often trustworthy. But when data from other sources are used, it is always necessary to carefully examine how the data were collected. The assessment of data quality is, again, a task for which evaluators are eminently qualified. Some of this expertise is technical and some comes from experience. For example, as a technical matter, good evaluators know well the assets of probability samples. And as a practical matter, good evaluators learn how to judge the quality of the plans that guide data collection. Data collected with clear and important uses in mind will usually be better than data collected as a mere formality. Thus, prison administrative records may be useful for documenting the quality of existing prison conditions. But, although such records can be quite accurate about which inmates have violated prison rules, they usually cannot be trusted to accurately indicate which inmates have engaged in exemplary behavior.

Quite often, existing data sources will provide contradictory estimates on any issue. But even chaos can sometimes be reduced to some order. Seemingly contradictory data on the same topic collected by opposing stakeholders can be especially useful for needs-assessment purposes. For example, both the Coalition Against Handguns and the National Rifle Association (NRA) have sponsored sample surveys of the American population concerning their approval or disapproval of gun control legislation. Although the reports issued by the Coalition and the NRA differed widely in their conclusions—with one finding much popular support for more stringent gun control measures and the other the opposite, respectively—a close inspection of the data showed that many of the specific findings were nearly identical in the two surveys (Wright, Rossi, and Daly 1983). Those findings on which both surveys agreed substantially could be taken with greater credibility.

In many instances, there may be no existing information that can be used to provide estimates of the extent and distribution of a problem. For example, it is likely that there are no sources of information about how households use pesticides or about the level of popular knowledge concerning how such substances can be safely deployed. Any instance of household pesticide misuse constitutes a problem, but how serious the problem is for, say, households with children present, may be unclear. Moreover, the precise content of the problem may be obscure. Perhaps households lack knowledge about the toxic properties of certain pesticides or, alternatively, they lack knowledge about other ways to control household or garden pests. Ordinarily there are no data sources from which information on such issues can be obtained. Under these circumstances, an evaluator may wish to undertake a preliminary study to estimate the amount and distribution of household pesticide use and knowledge about pesticides' toxic properties.

There are several ways of making such estimates of "need." Perhaps the easiest to undertake, but also the least reliable, is to collect "expert" testimony. Most of the larger estimates of the size of the homeless population are essentially compilations of local "experts' " guesses of the numbers of homeless in their localities. (See U.S. Conference of Mayors 1987.) Another information source that can be reliable, but often unavailable, is records from organizations that provide services to the population in question. For example, the extent of drug abuse in America may be extrapolated from the records of persons treated in hospital emergency rooms, assembled in the Drug Abuse Warning Network. Insofar as a consistent and known fraction of drug users go to hospitals with drug-related health emergencies, such data may be quite accurate.

In many cases, it may be necessary to undertake quite elaborate research in order to assess the size and distribution of some problem. To illustrate, the Robert Wood Johnson Foundation and the Pew Memorial Trust were trying to plan a program for increasing the access of homeless persons to medical care. Although there was ample evidence that serious medical conditions existed among the homeless populations in urban centers, there was virtually no precise information on either the size of the homeless population or the extent of the medical problems in that population. Hence, the foundations funded a research project to devise technical advances needed in sample survey methods to collect the missing information. The result was a study that influenced most of the subsequent research on homelessness and led to changes in plans for the 1990 census, making it possible to arrive at reasonable estimates of the homeless population on a national basis (Rossi 1989).

Needs assessment research is usually not as elaborate as the pilot research described previously. In many cases, straightforward sample surveys can provide most of the information necessary. For example, in planning for educational campaigns to increase public understanding of the risks associated with hazardous substances, it would be necessary to have a good understanding of what the current level of public knowledge is and which population subgroups pose special problems. A national sample survey would provide the necessary information.

The number of local needs assessments covering single municipalities, towns, or counties done every year must now be in the thousands. For example, the 1974 Community Mental Health legislation called for community mental health needs assessments to be undertaken periodically. The 1987 McKinney Act, mandating aid to the homeless, called for states and local communities to undertake needs assessments as the basis for planning programs for the homeless. Environmental impact statements to be prepared in advance of large-scale alterations in land use often call for impact estimates not just on various species of plants and animals, but also on public health and the local economy.

The quality of such local needs assessments varies widely but is most likely quite poor on the average. Especially difficult obstacles lie in the requirement to devise valid measurements of relatively subtle problems (e.g., distrust of food additives, mental health). For such problems, unusually high-quality surveying methods are essential.

Unfortunately, the necessary time, talent, and resources are rarely available at the local level either to field such work or even to make good decisions about outsiders to hire.

Despite our emphasis on things one can count, needs assessments do not have to be undertaken solely with quantitative techniques. Qualitative research, ranging in complexity from interviewing a few persons through group discussion sessions (as in focus groups) to more elaborate ethnographic fieldwork, may also be instructive, especially in getting detailed knowledge of the specific nature of the needs in question. For example, the development of educational campaigns may be considerably aided by qualitative data on the structure of popular beliefs. What, for instance, are the trade-offs people believe exist between the pleasures of cigarette smoking and the resulting health risks? An especially attractive feature of qualitative approaches is that they are sometimes inexpensive. Certainly, conducting three or four focus group sessions is cheaper than conducting the usual sample survey. Findings from focus group research may be especially instructive if groups members are unusually knowledgeable informants, who have access to information that ordinary citizens would not. For example, the problems that an emergency room might be serving large numbers of low-income patients might be best articulated by emergency room doctors and nurses and by key administrators in that hospital. A haphazard cross section of citizens would have little concrete information to offer.

However, qualitative approaches can be very expensive if they mean placing several researchers in the field for a number of months. For example, a study of the job training needs of low-income single parents (primarily women) might require two ethnographers and 6 months of fieldwork. The cost of the project would then be one person-year of effort from two highly trained anthropologists plus their research expenses (including travel, food, and lodging). The total bill could easily top $100,000. (See Edin and Lein 1997 for an example of an elaborate large-scale ethnographic study of welfare mothers and their sources of income.)

Although needs-assessment research is ordinarily undertaken for the descriptive purpose of developing accurate estimates of the amounts and distribution of a given problem, needs assessments can also yield some understanding of the underlying mechanisms. For example, a search for information on how many high school students study a non-English language may reveal that many schools do not offer such courses; part of the problem is that opportunities to learn foreign languages are insufficient. Or the fact that many primary school children of low socioeconomic backgrounds appear to be tired and listless in class may be explained by a finding that many did not eat breakfast before coming to school. Carefully and sensitively conducted qualitative studies are particularly important for uncovering process information of this sort. Thus ethnographic studies of disciplinary problems within high schools may suggest why some schools have fewer disciplinary problems than others, in addition to providing some indication of how widespread disciplinary problems are. The findings on why schools differ might suggest useful ways in which new programs could be designed. Or qualitative research on household energy consumption may reveal that few residents had any information on the energy-consumption characteristics of their appliances. Not knowing how they consume energy, household members cannot develop efficient strategies for reducing consumption.

Indeed, the history of ups and downs of public concern for social problems provides many examples of how qualitative studies (e.g., Carson 1955; Lewis 1965; Liebow 1967; Riis 1890), and sometimes novels (e.g., Sinclair 1906; Steinbeck 1939), have raised public consciousness about particular social problems. Sometimes the works in question are skillful combinations of qualitative and quantitative information, as in the case of Harrington (1962), whose *The Other America* contained much publicly available data interlaced with graphic descriptions of the living conditions endured by the poor.

Finally, for program planning purposes, it is usually important to be able to project current circumstances into the future. A problem that is serious at present, for instance, may be more or less serious years later. Indeed, it is the future that people really care about, because nothing can be done about the present anyway.

Typically, future projections are made in loose, qualitative terms. At least in the near term, the present situation is assumed to continue into the future. But sometimes, more sophisticated forecasting procedures are employed.

There are basically two kinds of forecasting approaches (Berk and Cooley 1987). One kind is really nothing more than fancy extrapolation.

There is no attempt to represent the causal mechanisms involved; statistical tools are used to "fit" historical data, and the fit is essentially carried forward into the future. Past trends are assumed to persist. Box-Jenkins time series models are one illustration. Models of this sort can often do very well in the short term. A second kind of model attempts to represent the causal mechanisms that generated the data. If prices, for instance, are being forecasted, key features of the relevant markets are included. Such structural models are more difficult to construct than extrapolation models, but if well done, they perform better over the longer term. Conventional regression formulations can be adapted to this purpose.

It is an old saying that only hindsight is exact. In fact, forecasting future trends can be quite risky, especially as the time horizon lengthens. There are also serious complications when there are scale changes, either in time or in space. For example, a procedure designed to forecast crime rates for entire states year by year may fail miserably if forecasts are made for counties within states on a monthly basis. One reason is that although penal code statutes are applied statewide, law enforcement occurs at the county or city level. As a result, the social processes generating crime statistics for counties or cities differ from those generating crime statistics at the state level. A good example is hate crimes, where despite a single statewide statute, some municipalities may have a special hate crime police unit and some may not.

At the most fundamental level, all forecasts depend on the assumption that the future will be much like the past. For example, a projection of the number of persons aged 18 to 30 a decade later at first blush seems easy to construct; the number of persons of that age 10 years hence is almost completely determined by the current age structure of the population. However, had demographers in central Africa made such a forecast 15 years ago, they would have been substantially off the mark. They would have failed to anticipate the tragic impact of the AIDS epidemic, which is affecting young adults most heavily. Projections with longer time horizons would have been even more problematic because trends in fertility as well as mortality would have to have been included.

We are not arguing against forecasting. Rather, we are concerned about uncritical acceptance of forecasts without a thorough examination of how the forecasts were produced. Examining the forecasting assumptions, for example, is a task that can range considerably in complexity. For simple extrapolations of existing trends, the assumptions may be relatively few and easily ascertained. But even if the assumptions are known, it is often unclear how to determine if the assumptions are reasonably met. For the kinds of projections developed from multiple-equation computer models, examining the assumptions may require the skills of an advanced programmer, several scientists with the relevant substantive knowledge, and a sophisticated statistician. Beyond the substantive assumptions, there are often a host of mathematical and algorithmic issues, because such computer models are at best rough approximations of what would ideally be needed. A key case in point are the computer models used to forecast climate scenarios under global warming (Barron 1995).

Whatever the source and credibility of the forecast, however, all forecasts should be reported as both point and interval estimates. The former is typically a single "best" guess, whereas the latter is a range of values in which the true (future) value likely lies. Unfortunately, for a large number of forecasting models, it is not apparent how a proper confidence interval may be constructed. Once again, climate models are an instructive illustration.

Stage 3: Can We Do Anything About the Problems? Problem-Driven Research

Diagnosis may be the first step on the road to treatment. The second step is understanding enough about the problem and its setting to devise appropriate remedies. That is, knowing a lot about the distribution and extent of a problem does not by itself lead automatically to solutions. In order to design programs, one must call on two sorts of knowledge. First, one needs valid knowledge on the leverage points and interventions useful for changing the distribution and extent of a problem. Second, one needs to know from a variety of sources something about the institutional arrangements that are implicated so that workable policies and programs can be designed.

For example, applied research in microeconomics has shown repeatedly that consumers typically will respond to price changes. Other things being equal, they will generally buy less of a commodity if its price increases. This lesson can be applied to conservation of all sorts. Yet it has been virtually impossible in many states to institute marginal cost pricing for water because of political opposition from large agricultural users, who, under existing schemes, are being subsidized by residential and industrial users (Berk et al. 1981).

To take another illustration from water conservation, applied research in social psychology indicates that people who are likely to conserve believe that others drawing on the same resource are conserving as well. Yet it is unclear how water consumers who believe that other consumers typically are not conserving can be convinced that they are not alone in their support for conservation efforts. The only consumption data they typically see are their own (on their bills). One strategy employed by some water districts in California has been to enclose in each consumer bill a short newsletter reporting aggregate trends in consumption for important segments of the community (Berk et al. 1981).

It cannot be overemphasized that to construct a program likely to be adopted by an organization, one needs to know how to introduce new procedures that would be undertaken with sufficient effort. Large organizations—schools, factories, social agencies, and the like—are resistant to change, especially when the changes are not reflected in the reward systems. For example, an educational program that is likely to work has to provide positive incentives for school systems, particular schools, and individual teachers. In short, inadequate attention to the organizational contexts of programs is one of the more frequent sources of program implementation failure. Mandating a program for an agency that is insufficiently motivated, poorly prepared, or lacking in the necessary skills is a sure recipe for degraded interventions. Indeed, under such circumstances, it is possible that no programs at all will be initiated; an organization that cannot deliver will not deliver.

The conception of policy-driven research we have just outlined apparently causes considerable misunderstanding about the relationships between basic and applied social research. Policy-driven research tries to determine how changes in policy can affect the phenomenon in question. In contrast, knowledge about the phenomenon per se (the province of basic disciplinary concerns) may have no ready links to what can be done about it. For example, a study finding convincingly that violent criminals often were abused as children does not in itself lead to rehabilitation programs for violent criminals or to concrete interventions in the homes of abused children. However, such a study might stimulate ideas for the kinds of policy-driven research necessary to develop sensible responses. That is, basic research may provide general clues about where and how to intervene.

Stage 4: Developing Promising Ideas
Into Promising Programs

Moving from a conception of what may be done to a program is the next step. The act of transforming promising ideas into a set of concrete activities is essentially the practice of art rather than science. Moreover, because the knowledge required is primarily substantive, evaluators may have no clear or necessary role. However, evaluators are more likely to make important contributions in the translation of ideas to programs insofar as they have a good understanding of the workings of similarly conceived past programs and of the capabilities of organizations likely to implement the program in question. Such information can come from three related sources: the evaluators' own "clinical" experience in similar situations, a careful review of the relevant literature, and a formal meta-analysis of the impact of other comparable programs. The importance of past experience and a careful literature review should be readily apparent. We can postpone a discussion of meta-analysis until the next chapter with little loss for the issues at hand.

To help make the key concepts clear, consider, for example, the energy crisis of the late 1970s. At that time, a needs assessment revealed that consumers had little specific knowledge of how their use of electrical appliances affected energy consumption. Of course, nearly every consumer knew that keeping refrigerator doors closed saved electricity and that turning off electrical burners when not being used for cooking would lower electricity consumption. However, few knew that there was wide variation in the energy used by different brands of refrigerators and electrical stoves. Needs assessment research also showed that most consumers were quite concerned about energy costs. In short, there was a reservoir of motivation to adopt energy conservation measures and substantial gaps in popular knowledge about how best to conserve.

Given these circumstances, there were a variety of programs that could have been developed, some resting on pricing changes that would have rewarded consumers for using appliances less during high-demand periods of the day and others based on educational efforts urging consumers to lower their thermostat settings. Furthermore, within each of these broad categories of programs, there were a variety of specific measures. Pricing schemes, for instance, might be built on the marginal price, the average price, increasing block pricing, and so on. Any pricing scheme based on units of consumption could proceed only if energy consumption could be accurately measured (e.g., by meters). In an ideal situation, the energy consumption for different appliances should be monitored so that, in principle, consumers could determine which appliances were especially inefficient (e.g., toasters) or inappropriately used (e.g., ovens used for heating a room). As a compromise, perhaps energy use could be metered by room. And finally, means would be necessary to inform consumers about their energy consumption in ways that effectively communicated the consequences of how they used appliances; rapid and accurate feedback would be an essential part of the program and, ideally, appliance-by-appliance breakdowns should be provided.

The point is that programs are a set of activities undertaken by individuals and organizations. Specifying these details is a very long way from the broad ideas about possible interventions, and it requires nuts-and-bolts knowledge of past programs and current prospects. In the energy consumption example just given, an evaluator, it is hoped, would know a lot about a large number of earlier conservation programs and about the day-to-day functioning of the local utility company. Note, however, that such knowledge is primarily substantive and hardly the sole preserve of evaluation researchers.

In contrast, evaluators should feel right at home with pilot studies. Although we know of no clear and compelling definition of a pilot study in a program evaluation context, perhaps the most useful conception of pilot studies emphasizes the explicitly provisional nature of the intervention being researched. That is, there is a tentative commitment to a loosely defined program, but program developers are consciously agnostic about a host of details on which data may well shed some light. Continuing with the energy conservation example, pilot studies might be undertaken to see how different pricing mechanisms might be instituted and whether there is any evidence that they might work. Thus, if consumers are to pay a higher per-unit price as the amount consumed increases (e.g., under increasing block pricing), there must be some assurance that consumers understand their electric bills and the links between how they use appliances and the amount of electricity that is consumed. These are the kinds of tasks by which evaluators earn their keep.

Likewise, evaluation skills per se are not especially relevant for the translation of broad conceptions of educational television programs into the scripts, lighting, directing, filming, and editing of "Mr. Rogers' Neighborhood." However, evaluators can play an essential role in the pilot testing (pretesting) of such television programs. For example, useful educational programs must demonstrate that they can get the attention of their intended audiences, be understood by them, and produce predispositions to act in desired fashions. Thus, pilot versions of new programs are often tested on small audiences whose responses are carefully monitored. Elements of a program that repel audiences, lead to misunderstanding, or lead to undesired behavior can be changed. Then the program can be finely tuned until pretest audience responses are acceptable. In practice, useful pilot studies can fall short of full scientific rigor, for instance, using pretest television audiences that are selected haphazardly. Or pilot studies can involve rigorous research programs that would do a major university proud.

Toward the less rigorous side of the continuum, pretesting is routinely undertaken by the Children's Television Workshop, producers of "Sesame Street." The producers employ volunteer pretest audiences of preschoolers to measure the attention-getting abilities of its episodes. The producers watch how closely pretest audiences follow the action of the episode being tested. In addition, the audience is interviewed after each showing to ascertain whether or not the message of the program was understood clearly. Program deficiencies are then rectified, and the process is repeated until a program acceptable to the producers is finally achieved.

Another example, the Lodge Program developed by Fairweather and his associates (Fairweather and Tornatsky 1977), employed very rigorous pilot-testing procedures. The goal was to return mental patients to noninstitutionalized life in a way that would reduce the chances of being rehospitalized. Drawing on social science findings about the importance of informal supports within small groups, Fairweather and his colleagues took two decades to develop a technique based on constructing small groups of patients eligible for discharge that could be used by most mental hospitals and that was demonstrably effective in lowering the return rates. The development process consisted of a series of randomized field experiments in which version after version of the program was tested until an effective version was achieved.

Sometimes pilot studies do not require fielding a provisional version of the program. It is interesting to note that computer simulations may be used instead, at least for certain kinds of programs. For example, the California Department of Corrections is considering a revision of the means by which inmates are assigned to prison housing (Berk and de Leeuw 1997). For more than a decade, inmates had been assigned through a scoring system based on information collected at intake. Background factors, such as age, thought to be associated with a higher risk of misconduct in prison, were given standard weights and then summed. (Younger inmates are more likely to cause problems.) The higher the score, the higher the projected risk. The summed scores were then used to make housing assignments so that higher scores meant placement in more secure facilities.

Recently, under pressure to use prison space more efficiently, the California Department of Corrections has considered a number of revisions of its scoring and placement system. However, the revisions could not be allowed to allocate more inmates to particular facilities than those facilities could safely contain. As a consequence, computer programs were written to simulate the implications of different scoring and placement systems for the distribution of inmates across different prisons. The task was difficult because, over time, incarcerated inmates leave the system, new inmates arrive, and inmates move between different prisons based on how they behave. Still, one can think of the simulations as pilot studies for different scoring and placement systems.

Another pilot-testing strategy not requiring a provisional version of the program is to ask people how they would respond to some hypothetical program. Perhaps the most common way this is done is through sample surveys. For example, it is common in market research to ask respondents about how much they like different versions of possible products. Automobile manufacturers, for instance, will ask potential buyers which options they would be prepared to purchase at given prices. Similarly, utilities companies will ask their customers about the acceptability of different rebate programs, the goal of which is to motivate homeowners to retrofit with water- and energy-saving appliances (Berk and Shulman 1995b). Thorough pilot testing during the development phase can increase the chances that a worthwhile program will emerge. But it is one thing to have a program that works well with test participants and quite another to have a program that will work well with real participants. For example, a "Sesame Street" episode that does well in a studio atmosphere has none of the competition for attention that exists in an ordinary living room. Indeed, an adult-oriented health information program, "Feeling Good," that was developed by the Children's Television Workshop did well with pretest audiences but failed to achieve significant audience shares when aired on public television stations during prime viewing hours. The test audiences in the studios liked the episodes they viewed, but the unconstrained audience preferred programs on other channels that were competing with "Feeling Good."

Stage 5: The YOAA Problem

Once a prospective program has been refined through pilot studies, the time comes to transport the program to a more realistic operating environment. However, moving from the development phase to the operational phase usually means transferring responsibility from a research-oriented organization to an operating agency. This leads to the "Can YOAA Do It?" problem. Translation: Can "your ordinary American agency" carry out the program with fidelity? It is well-known that in such settings, Murphy's Law surely applies: If anything can go wrong, it will. But it also seems that if anything cannot go wrong, it will too.

Often the YOAA problem has been identified with the character of large-scale bureaucracies, a diagnosis that obscures as much as it illuminates. The issue is whether an operating agency has the appropriately trained personnel, a sufficiently motivating reward system, and the resources to carry out a program at the desired level of fidelity. Asking an already overburdened agency to take on additional work, especially work for which its personnel are not trained, is clearly a recipe for failure. For example, an emergency room program for counseling crime victims, developed in a major Los Angeles hospital, was never implemented because social workers paid by the program were actually used to reduce shortages of social workers in the wards. State public welfare agencies are currently struggling with the new definitions of their tasks imposed by the reforms enacted under the Personal Responsibility and Work Obligation Reconciliation Act passed by Congress in 1996. Under the previous legislation, welfare workers primarily worked on determining the eligibility of poor households for welfare benefits. Under the new legislation, state welfare agencies have to assume the responsibilities of moving individuals into the labor force, providing job training and remedial education as well as providing access to employment. These changes require different skills and different activities. Some research has already shown that welfare workers are not performing very well in their new tasks (Meyers, Glaser, and MacDonald 1998).

In addition, even agencies with the requisite resources and skill may in practice "drop the ball" because of some legitimate confusion, incomplete communication, insufficient follow-through, or a host of effectively unpredictable difficulties. For example, an experimental program in Colorado Springs, Colorado, to test different policing strategies in domestic violence incidents was at first poorly implemented because of a totally unrelated strike threatened by rank-and-file officers who were seeking bargaining rights for their union. Fortunately, program implementation improved dramatically when the issues underlying the threatened strike were effectively resolved (Berk et al. 1992).

Therefore, it is vital to study how programs are implemented, and descriptive accounts may be especially valuable. For example, a program designed to keep teenage mothers in school relied on the school systems to report attendance of young women subject to the program (Bloom et al. 1991). Mothers who had unexcused absences were to be sanctioned by lowered benefits. The program was unable to obtain from schools consistent compliance with reporting requirements. As a result, sanctions were rarely applied when mothers neglected to attend schools: The program was never fully implemented. Similarly, a program designed to allow the use of food stamps by homeless persons in soup kitchens was never implemented correctly because there was no incentive for the homeless to apply for and use food stamps to "purchase" the free food. Furthermore, soup kitchens refused to accept food stamps because doing so would jeopardize their eligibility for free food supplies under surplus commodity distribution programs (Burt and Cohen 1989).

It is at this point that it may make some sense to initiate demonstration programs in which operating agencies attempt to implement the program. Demonstration programs can be viewed as another developmental step when attention is centered on the problems that operating agencies encounter carrying out a program. A prime example is the administrative experiment (a misnomer because these demonstrations were not truly experiments) carried out in connection with a proposed housing voucher program. Ten municipalities were selected to work out procedures for administering housing-voucher programs in their localities and to carry them out for a period of years. The demonstrations were closely monitored by researchers, who carefully noted all the difficulties each of the ten cities encountered in administering their versions of the housing-voucher program (Struyk and Bendick 1981).

Stage 6: Will a Particular Program Work?
The Effectiveness Issue

After a program has been fine-tuned and its operational kinks have been ironed out through demonstrations, there still remains the question of effectiveness. To this point, all one has managed to do is document that the program in question can be implemented with sufficient fidelity as a prototype. It is important to realize that effectiveness goes far beyond implementation and revolves around whether a program produces the changes anticipated. Recall, also, that effectiveness may be relative or marginal, and may take cost into account.

Effectiveness is rarely obvious for at least two reasons. First, it is often difficult to distinguish program effects from the effects of other major forces affecting the outcome. We addressed this earlier under internal validity. Second, it is often difficult to distinguish program effects from chance variation, which, as "noise," may mask any program impact. We addressed this earlier in discussing statistical conclusion validity. And both problems are exacerbated by interventions that are typically weak and, for that reason, unlikely to produce strong effects.

Why most interventions are weak raises issues beyond the scope of this book (Rossi 1987). Nevertheless, among the most important explanations is that the social environments in which interventions are likely to be introduced are usually shaped by a large number of forces. Yet the programs introduced rarely address more than one of these. Nutritional behavior, for example, is affected by upbringing, ethnic background, disposable income, local availability of food products, information about nutritional issues, subjective estimates of risks to health and well-being for the nutritional behavior in question, household composition, the nutritional practices of family members and peers, chemical dependencies, and many other influences. Yet programs meant to improve nutrition rarely target more than one of the possible influences. To make matters worse, there appears to be no single developmental stage that, if interrupted, will improve nutritional practices effectively. In short, there are many ways to affect eating habits, but each by itself is a small part of the picture.

When a promising program has been identified, and a reasonable working version developed, the next step is to see whether the program is effective enough to justify its becoming a routine part of some agency's activities. At this point, we recommend the use of randomized experiments to test the effectiveness of candidate programs. Recall that we earlier spoke of randomized experiments as the gold standard for internal validity. Later, a wider range of design will be discussed when we turn to evaluation of ongoing programs. Because the alternatives to random assignment are typically less desirable for causal inference, randomized experiments should be the design of choice when random assignment can be properly implemented. The desirable situation is far more likely to exist when new programs are being developed than when an ongoing program must be assessed, and so we will consider quasi-experiments later.

Randomized experiments are desirable (some would say mandatory—see Boruch 1997 and Berk et al. 1985 for examples), because randomly allocating persons (or other units, such as classes) to an experimental group or to a control group ensures that all the factors ordinarily affecting the outcome in question are, on the average, distributed identically across those who receive the program and those who do not. Therefore, randomization, on the average, prevents the confounding of estimated treatment effects with the impact of other factors that may affect the outcome. As a result, internal validity is enhanced enormously, and the likelihood of reporting spurious causal effects is dramatically reduced. Equally important, randomization also means that the conditions for valid statistical inference are likely to be met without the need for any further assumptions or dependence on large samples. In the randomization process, one can find the gold standard for statistical conclusion validity as well as the gold standard for internal validity (Good 1993; Rosenbaum 1995, chap. 2; Rubin 1978).

However, this commitment in no way undermines the complementary potential of qualitative approaches such as ethnographic studies, particularly to document why a particular intervention succeeds or fails. For example, in designing educational campaigns based on workshops, qualitative studies can uncover those organizations in which implementation may be most easily achieved. Thus, workshops held for employees after 5:00 p.m. may appear to be an efficient strategy except that interviews with employees could reveal that few would remain after work for any purpose.

Developmental experiments should ordinarily be conducted on a relatively modest scale and are most useful for policy when they test a range of alternative programs that are intended to achieve the *same* effects. For example, it might be useful for an experiment to test several ways of motivating people to have their homes tested for radon because the findings could be used to provide information on the relative effectiveness of several attractive (a priori) methods. Likewise, an experiment on a range of policing strategies in domestic violence incidents, such as making arrests, providing restraining orders, offering crisis counseling, and giving citations, would be more instructive than an experiment that considers only two alternatives.

There are many good examples of field testing promising programs through randomized experiments (see Boruch 1997 for examples), and even many instances in which promising programs were studied with a series of randomized experiments. The five income maintenance experiments were devised to test, under varying conditions, the impact of negative income tax plans as substitutes for existing welfare programs (Hausman and Wise 1985; Kershaw and Fair 1976; Robins et al. 1980; Rossi and Lyall 1974). The Department of Labor tested the extension of unemployment benefit coverage to prisoners released from state prisons in a small randomized experiment conducted in Baltimore (Lenihan 1976), and later extended the research to the states of Texas and Georgia (Rossi, Berk, and Lenihan 1980). Randomized experiments have also been used to test national health insurance plans and direct cash subsidies for housing to poor families (Struyk and Bendick 1981). In the environmental area, six alternative approaches to communicating information about radon were tested in New York (Smith et al. 1987). The Minneapolis Spouse Abuse Experiment, which tested three different policing strategies in domestic violence incidents, was replicated in six new field experiments in six different cities (Berk et al. 1992). The recent spate of welfare reforms has been informed by a number of randomized experiments undertaken in California and elsewhere (Gueron and Pauly 1991; Handler 1995; Riccio et al. 1994). Perhaps the most extended series of developmental experiments was undertaken by Fairweather and Tornatzky (1977), comprising more than two decades of consistent refinement and retesting and resulting in a replicable, effective treatment that could be implemented under a variety of conditions.

Given a program of proven effectiveness, the next question one might reasonably raise is whether the opportunity costs of the program are justified by the gains achieved. Or the same question might be more narrowly raised in a comparative framework: Is Program A more "efficient" than Program B, both otherwise equally acceptable alternative ways of achieving some particular goal?

The main problem in answering such questions centers on establishing a yardstick by which comparisons may be made. For example, would it be more useful to divide the units of achievement gained by dollars, the number of students covered, or the number of classes served by the program? In fact, usually the most convenient way to define efficiency is to calculate cost-effectiveness: the number of dollars spent per unit of output. In the case of "Sesame Street," for example, two cost-effectiveness measures were computed: (1) dollars spent per child-hour of viewing, a measure of the cost of running the program; and (2) dollars spent per each additional letter of the alphabet learned, a cost-effectiveness measure taking into account increases in learning (Cook et al. 1975). Note that the second measure implies knowing the impact of the program, presumably from a formal impact assessment.

The most complicated way of addressing the efficiency question is to conduct a full-fledged benefit-cost analysis in which all of the values of all of the benefits and costs are computed. The ratio of benefits to costs is the benefit-cost ratio of the program. However, relatively few full-fledged benefit-cost analyses have been conducted for social programs because it is difficult to convert all the costs and all the benefits into the same metric. In principle, it is possible to convert into dollars all program costs and benefits. In practice, however, it is rarely possible to do so because of disagreements over the value of various program inputs and outputs. For example, it would be difficult to affix a dollar value to learning an additional letter of the alphabet.

A second problem with full-fledged benefit-cost analyses is that they must consider the long-run consequences of the program in question and the long-run consequences for the next best alternative forgone. This immediately raises the question of how to value, in today's dollars, future returns from some investment. The usual assumption is that current consumption is worth more than future consumption (in part because of delayed gratification), so that a dollar's worth of some commodity consumed today is worth less than a dollar's worth consumed in the future. This process is called "discounting." So far so good.

But in the context of program evaluation, the future returns (benefits minus costs) of alternative interventions need to be compared *after* discounting. For example, an assessment of a vocational training program in inner-city high schools needs to consider (among many other things) the long-run impact of the program on students' earnings over their lifetimes. At the very least, this means valuing in today's dollars the lifetime earnings of the individuals receiving vocational training and the lifetime earnings of individuals receiving the next best alternative. One difficulty is the need to forecast earnings into a future in which labor markets likely will be very different from today. However, our main point is that a discount rate must be determined, and the discount rate depends in part on interest rates decades in the future. One only has to look back over the past decade to see how volatile interest rates can be. Recall, also, our earlier discussion on the difficulties of forecasting.

For these and other reasons, choosing the discount rate is usually a judgment call. As a result, the discount rate for any given evaluation is often the source of controversy (Thompson 1980), especially when the reported success or failure of a program may depend on the discount rate chosen. Perhaps the most visible current illustration is the debate over alternative means to respond to global warming. The time horizon is more than 100 years, and the value taken as the discount rate can determine whether it is better to dramatically cut greenhouse gas emission over the next decade or essentially do nothing now and then pay for the cost of adapting to the climate change that is likely to follow.

To summarize, the conceptual framework of benefit-cost analysis is often useful because it forces stakeholders to confront the painful fact that all social programs have opportunity costs in both the short and the long run. In addition, phrasing program outcomes in cost-effectiveness terms is often a handy method for addressing the trade-offs between alternative programs. But a detailed benefit-cost analysis is typically impractical, and one must be very cautious of claims derived from such exercises. One often has the feeling that for such analyses, reality is a special case.

Practical Developmental Evaluation Approaches

If all of the research activities described in the preceding pages were undertaken for each and every proposed program or policy shift, the pace of change in American public programs would be appreciably slowed. Thus, although one must admire the devotion, care, and diligence of Fairweather and his colleagues, when the Lodge approach had finally been perfected, psychopharmacological developments and the community mental health movement had so drastically changed the treatment of mental health patients that the Lodge approach had become largely irrelevant. While Fairweather and his associates labored carefully and at great length to perfect the Lodge approach, the content of policy space had shifted to highlight other concerns about the treatment of mentally ill individuals.

Clearly, practical approaches to program development have to take into account all the constraints on time and resources that are ordinarily confronted. Decades-long development efforts may be the "right" way, but the practical way must deliver the best possible information in a timely fashion. There are no hard and fast guidelines about how best to proceed, although a few broad principles may be stated.

In general, judgments about whether to evaluate a program, and about how thorough that evaluation must be, should rest, at least in principle, on a rough benefit-cost ratio for the proposed evaluation. That is, one must place some value on the information that could be obtained under different evaluation designs. Other things being equal, the greater the potential impact of the proposed program—whether it succeeds or fails—the more carefully it should be evaluated. This means that programs that promise to be costly, that may have adverse and widespread effects, or that deal with the central, gnawing problems of society probably deserve the best possible evaluation. Programs in which the consequences of an ineffective program are slight may typically warrant far less attention. Indeed, there is no doubt that some programs need not be scrutinized at all. Before proceeding, however, it is vital to factor in what kinds of evaluations are feasible, how credible their results are likely to be, and what each would cost to undertake. A very important program, such as Social Security, may be prohibitively expensive to evaluate persuasively. Alternatively, an evaluation of a community's efforts to reduce bicycle accidents, by instituting inspections of bicycles ridden to local schools, may produce a lot of useful information per dollar spent.

Finally, the evaluative activities in support of program development have been described earlier as a set of procedures arrayed over time. We emphasize again that this need not be the case. A set of experiments conducted simultaneously on several alternative programs can reduce the total time needed to arrive at useful conclusions. Demonstrations of programs can be used for fine-tuning purposes. Randomized experiments may be foregone when there are very strong indications of effectiveness from nonexperimental evidence. Although there is an expositional logic to the chronology presented and a thoroughness that follows when each stage is executed in the order proposed, we are offering no recipe. Evaluation practitioners in real time and on site will always have to make judgment calls.

4

Examining Ongoing Programs

A Chronological Perspective

Once a program has been enacted and is functioning, one of the main questions is whether the program is functioning *properly*. Attention is directed not to whether the program is achieving its intended effects but to whether the program is operating day to day as expected. Often explicit is a comparison between the program as designed and the program as it is actually implemented.

For example, even well-planned programs often have to be fine-tuned in the first few months of operation. Indeed, estimates of effectiveness should be made only when any necessary "shakedown period" is over. For example, one of the criticisms of the Fort Bragg Experiment on managed mental health care services (Bickman, Summerfelt, and Noser 1997) was that the evaluation was done too early in the program's evolution: It was judged before it had reached operational efficiency.

Stage 1: Is the Program Reaching the Appropriate Beneficiaries?

Achieving appropriate coverage of beneficiaries is often problematic. Sometimes a program is so poorly designed that it simply does not reach significant portions of the total intended beneficiary population. For example, an educational program designed to reach intravenous drug users through community institutions such as churches and schools may simply miss its target population, most of whom do not use those community institutions. Likewise, a federal program to provide food subsidies to home day care facilities for children of poor families was found to serve mainly children who were not poor (Glantz et al. 1997).

In addition, patterns of the problem may change over time, sometimes in response to the existence of a program itself. For example, it is quite likely that the existence of shelters for battered women increases the demand for shelters (Rossi 1994). Among other things, shelters validate the option of leaving oppressive living arrangements. Another example concerns the labeling of consumer products. Labels printed in extremely small type or that use professional jargon may satisfy agency regulations; they may also be ignored by most consumers. The labeling program simply does not reach many of its intended beneficiaries. In short, it is important to review from time to time how many of the intended beneficiaries are in fact being helped by a program.

Experience with social programs over the past three decades has shown that there are few, if any, programs that achieve full coverage or even near full coverage of intended beneficiaries, especially where coverage depends on actions that must be undertaken by prospective beneficiaries. Thus, not all persons who are eligible for Social Security payments actually apply for them; estimates indicate that up to 5% of all eligible beneficiaries never apply. The Food Stamp Program reaches about 80% of the families who are eligible (Rossi 1998b). Retail business can count on the fact that a large fraction of consumers who buy products offering mail-in rebates never bother to seek the rebates. And every state that has a lottery routinely has winning tickets that are never claimed.

There is also another side to the coverage problem. Programs may extend benefits to persons or organizations that were not intended beneficiaries. Such unwanted coverage may be impossible to avoid because of the ways in which the program is delivered. For example, although "Sesame Street" was designed primarily to reach disadvantaged children, it is also attractive to advantaged children and to their parents. There is no way to keep anyone from viewing a television program once it is broadcast (nor is it desirable to do so in this case), and hence a successful television program designed to reach some specific group of children may reach many others as well (Cook et al. 1975). Although the unintended viewers of "Sesame Street" are reached at no additional cost to broadcasters, there are times when unwanted coverage can severely drain program resources. For example, although Congress may have wished to provide educational experiences to returning veterans through the GI Bill and its successors, it was not clear whether Congress had in mind the subsidization of the many new proprietary educational enterprises that came into being primarily to supply "vocational" education to eligible veterans. Or, in the case of the bilingual education program, many primarily English-speaking children were found to be program beneficiaries because some school systems discovered that the special bilingual classes were an excellent place to tuck away their trouble-making English-speaking students.

Overcoverage is closely related to the free-rider problem, in which some beneficiaries get program benefits without having to bear their share of the costs. For example, homeowners who respond to utility company appeals by installing water-saving appliances and adopt low-water-use landscaping save water that is then available not just to other responsible citizens but to individuals who make no such investments. Free-riders not only raise questions of fairness, but can make programs inefficient and undermine the cooperation of individuals who are being exploited (Berk et al. 1981).

Studies designed to measure coverage are similar in principle to those discussed earlier under needs assessment studies. For example, a utility company might survey its customers to determine who is taking advantage of an advertised rebate for installing better home insulation. Or a telephone company might review its own records to see how many of its customers are taking advantage of "lifeline" rates. Or a university might examine its admissions records to determine if affirmative action programs are being applied inappropriately to noncovered minority groups (e.g., Asian Americans). Perhaps the main difference between coverage studies and needs assessments is that for the former there will more likely be systematic records on which to build. That is, the existence of a functioning program often implies the existence of program records with useful information.

Of course existing program records cover only those who have been served by a program. If the need is to find out about those who might benefit from the program but have not participated, surveys of likely members of the target population may become necessary. Such surveys can be quite expensive.

Stage 2: Is the Program Being Properly Delivered?
Program Integrity Research

It is far easier to describe a program than deliver it. Especially when program services depend heavily on the ability to recruit and train appropriate personnel, to retrain existing personnel, or to undertake significant changes in standard operating procedures, it is sometimes difficult to implement the intervention as designed. And one cannot always rule out incompetence or outright corruption. But whatever the reason, a program that is not delivered as it was intended subverts the earlier developmental effort and spends money on false pretenses.

Several examples may highlight the importance of program integrity. Although informational pamphlets on proper nutrition can be provided to medical personnel, pharmacies, and hospitals, the distribution of such literature to patients is always problematic. Properly motivating personnel to add the distribution of pamphlets to their existing duties is necessary but difficult to accomplish. And if the pamphlets are not delivered, there is no program. Likewise, when an educational program on birth control requires that special equipment be used, as in the case of the distribution of video- and audiocassettes, delivery of the program can be made problematic. In some cases, for instance, an assumption that schools have the requisite equipment to use these materials may be inaccurate.

In other situations, the anticipated services are delivered, but in diluted form. For example, a supplementary reading instruction program may be designed as an average of two instructional hours per student per week. However, in practice, 30 minutes of the program may be delivered on the average. The 75% reduction may lower reading gains proportionally, in which case the program's impact may be trivial. Or worse, the 75% reduction may drop the program below a threshold at which any gains occur.

Program integrity is often a particular problem in "loosely coupled" organizations in which the lines of authority are unclear or in which the lines of authority mean little in practice. Academic departments in universities are an excellent example. The professional autonomy given to professors and the tradition of academic freedom mean that department chairs often have little control over what is taught in classrooms. Many human service organizations—hospitals, police departments, courts, welfare departments, and secondary schools—have similar problems. In all such organizations, it is difficult to control what is occurring at the point of service delivery because of the discretion and autonomy given to service workers. To take another example, despite the threat of AIDS and other blood-transmitted diseases, it is often difficult to get emergency room nurses to always use surgical gloves when handling patients.

Program integrity can also be a serious problem when there is no agreement about what constitutes the program or about how program content should be measured. If there is no way to know empirically what program content should be, there is no way to determine if the right program is being delivered. It may seem strange that such programs could be launched, but ill-defined and ill-measured content is common in programs claiming to deliver "high-quality" mental health services. There is actually no consensus on what constitutes "high quality" or how best to measure it (Bickman and Salzer 1997). For example, there is no agreement about whether the protection of patients' rights should be included in measures of mental health service quality or whether it is really part of another issue.

Evaluation research designed to measure what is being delivered may be simple or complex. Thus, it may be very easy to learn from hospitals how many persons are served each week in their various outpatient services but very difficult to learn precisely what transpires in the interactions between medical personnel and patients. For example, if one is interested in the kinds of information provided by physicians and nurses in outpatient care, one would have to undertake an in-depth observational study that might well be very expensive to implement on a large scale. As another illustration, consider an evaluation of efforts to teach literacy as part of vocational training. One key question might be whether a particular pedagogical approach was being employed as promised. If only about six classes were being studied, two full-time observers would probably be needed to do classroom observation. In addition, there is always the possibility that the presence of observers may alter the behaviors of teachers and students.

One of the best examples of systematic studies in difficult-to-observe situations is Reiss's (1971) study of police-citizen encounters. Research assistants were assigned to ride with police on patrol and to systematically record each encounter between the police and members of the public. Reiss's study provides basic descriptive accounts of how such encounters are generated, how behavior of citizens affected police responses, and so on.

Another example of an excellent implementation study examined the mental hospitals that serve the Chicago metropolitan area (Lewis et al. 1987). The main problem was to describe how the legislation and rules for involuntary commitment to mental hospitals in place since the 1970s were working out in practice. The researchers discovered that fewer than 1% of the patients admitted over a year's time were involuntarily committed. Observing the court procedures, they found that many persons brought to the attention of the police because of their bizarre or aggressive behavior were offered the choice of voluntary commitment for up to 30 days or involuntary commitment for 60 days or more. The courts and prosecutors offered these alternatives because involuntary commitment involved lengthy procedures that could appreciably reduce the number of cases the court could process. Given the choice, most persons brought in under complaint chose the more lenient alternative. These practices averted what might potentially have been a great burden on the courts and prosecutors. However, the courts' procedures meant that stays in mental hospitals in Chicago were short and repeated frequently for those who were seriously mentally ill.

To fine-tune a program, it may not be necessary to collect data on a large scale. It may not matter, for instance, whether a particular implementation problem occurs frequently or infrequently, because it is not desirable for it to occur at all. Thus small-scale, qualitative observational studies may be most fruitful for program fine-tuning. For example, if qualitative interviews with welfare recipients reveal any instances in which husband-wife separations were undertaken solely for the purpose of retaining or increasing benefit eligibility, there might be sufficient evidence of the need to revise program eligibility rules penalizing intact husband and wife families.

Programs that depend heavily on particular personnel for delivery, that involve complicated activities, or that call for individualized treatments for beneficiaries are especially good candidates for careful and sensitive fine-tuning research. Such programs imply that the unique characteristics of program personnel coupled with the unique characteristics of beneficiaries effectively determine what is delivered. Because it is impossible to standardize the program, it is difficult to control what is delivered. Thus individualized human services are especially problematic. (See Fairweather and Tornatsky 1977 for an outstanding example.)

Stage 3: Are the Funds Being Used Appropriately?
Fiscal Accountability

The accounting profession has been around considerably longer than has program evaluation; procedures for determining whether program funds have been used responsibly and as intended are well established and, hence, are not problematic. However, assessments of fiscal accountability cannot substitute for the studies mentioned previously. Proper use of funds does not necessarily imply that program services are being delivered as intended. Conventional accounting categories used in fiscal audits are ordinarily sufficient to detect inappropriate or fraudulent expenditure patterns, but they may be insufficiently sensitive to detect whether services are being delivered to appropriate beneficiaries at the recommended levels. As described earlier, for instance, just because salaries of emergency room social workers were paid as required did not mean that the social workers were delivering the promised services. Recall that the social workers were commonly used on the wards instead of in the emergency room.

Recognizing that traditional accounting procedures could not address effectiveness issues, the General Accounting Office in the 1980s set up a special division, called the Program Evaluation and Methodology Division, one of whose major roles is to instruct GAO personnel in appropriate evaluation procedures and to undertake evaluations of programs at the request of Congress. A few years ago, the division was disbanded because evaluation methods had been successfully incorporated into the ordinary operations of the General Accounting Office. Still, one important caveat is necessary. Sometimes cost "containment" is a central concern by itself, with costs operationalized through usual accounting procedures. A good example is the controversy surrounding the Fort Bragg evaluation by Bickman and his colleagues over the effectiveness of managed mental health services (Bickman et al. 1995), where controlling costs was one of the outcomes addressed. That is, the issue of cost was a matter not of the proper use of funds, but of the program goals.

It is also important to keep in mind that the definition of costs under accounting principles differs from the definition of costs used by economists. For accountants, a cost reflects conventional bookkeeping entries such as out-of-pocket expenses, historical costs (i.e., what the purchase price of some item was), depreciation, and the like. Accountants focus on the value of current stocks of capital goods and inventories of products coupled with cash flow concerns. When the question is whether program funds are being appropriately spent, the accountants' definition will suffice. However, economists stress opportunity costs defined in terms of what is given up when resources are allocated to particular purposes. More specifically, opportunity costs reflect the next best use to which the resources could be put. For example, the opportunity cost of raising teachers' salaries by 10% may be the necessity of forgoing the purchase of a new set of textbooks. (Indeed, just such a case was recently reported for a school system in Orange County, California.) Although opportunity costs may not be especially important from a cost-accounting point of view, they become critical when cost-effectiveness or benefit-cost analyses of programs are undertaken. We will have more to say about these issues later.

Fiscal accountability and the two evaluation tasks discussed earlier in this chapter (beneficiaries served and program integrity) are directed mainly to how well a program is functioning. But whether or not a program is "effective" is a different question. Essentially, one must determine whether or not a program is achieving its goals over and above what would be expected if the program did not exist. Many evaluators consider estimates of effectiveness the quintessential evaluation task. We suspect that this derives in part from the laboratory roots of many evaluation research techniques. In the laboratory, the treatment and control conditions are usually under the control of the researcher and, as a consequence, are not problematic. The researcher knows what was being delivered to whom. The "real" question, therefore, becomes whether the treatment has any impact. However, social programs are not launched in laboratories, and program content is often the critical issue. Indeed, one could argue that unless there are ways to determine precisely what was delivered to whom, program impact is irrelevant: What good is it to know an effect without knowing its cause?

Suppose, for example, that one wanted to evaluate efforts to introduce literacy training into vocational training classes. Also suppose that vocational trainees are assigned at random to two classrooms, one of which is to teach the usual vocational content and one of which is to integrate literacy and vocational training. Finally, suppose that, although there are absolutely no data on what went on in the two classrooms (from either observation, accounts from students, or accounts from teachers or other sources), later reading scores for the integrated curriculum are far higher than for the vocational curriculum alone. That is, there is convincing evidence of program impact. However, without knowing about treatment content, what could possibly be done with the results? It is impossible, for instance, to use these results to justify routinizing the program, because no one but the students and teachers would have any idea what the program is. The question is: Routinize what?

This illustration conveys why, in our view, questions about how a program is functioning logically precede questions about program impact. An impact assessment is a waste of time unless the intervention is known and understood. Thus, there is certainly no justification for interpreting every evaluation task in effectiveness terms, as some evaluators have done in the past, spurred by imprecise requests for help from policymakers and administrators. Once the treatment is well documented, however, the success or failure of that program is quite properly addressed. The proverbial "bottom line" is always whether the program "works." We turn, then, to ways in which program effectiveness may be empirically examined.

Stage 4: Can Effectiveness Be Estimated?
The Evaluability Question

The effectiveness of a program that has gone through the stages described earlier in this chapter should, in principle, be an answerable empirical question. Put a bit more cautiously, an impact assessment should not be precluded. But there are many programs that present problems for effectiveness studies because one or more of the stages described earlier was neglected or handled poorly. Perhaps most important, an impact assessment is impossible without well-formulated program objectives. For example, a program designed to increase learning among certain groups of schoolchildren through the provision of supplemental per capita payments to schools is not evaluable without further specification of goals. "Increase learning" is hardly very specific. One would need to know such things as what sort of "learning" was to be included and what a nontrivial "increase" entailed.

Even biomedical experiments are not immune to vague goals. Freedman and Zeisel (1988) described testing the claims that a certain chemical is alleged to increase the risk of cancer, in which the researchers assumed that this claim could be evaluated with a randomized experiment using mice as subjects. A perplexing question soon presented itself: How should one define the outcome variables? Carcinogens are often rather specific in their impact; some may be associated with cancer of the liver and others with cancer of the lungs. For an experiment at hand, which cancers should be counted? If, for example, all cancers are counted, an apparent finding of "no effect" may be misleading. Small but important effects for a particular kind of cancer may be lost in the noise when all tumors are aggregated. In other words, the outcome should be stated in terms of the particular kinds of cancers anticipated, not cancer in general.

Clarifying goals can often be accomplished by helping program personnel to articulate them. This may mean hours of conversations over a number of weeks. For example, a program of workshops on domestic violence designed for judges might have as its initial goal "making judges more sensitive to family violence cases." But does this mean changing sentencing patterns, providing emotional support for victims through counselors, reducing the number of continuances (which are very hard on victims), or what? It might take several meetings among the evaluator, agency personnel, and the agency's advisory board before the program's goals were properly clarified. Yet this step is absolutely essential.

A second criterion for evaluability is that program content be well specified. Thus, a program "encouraging innovation" to make health education agencies more effective is not amenable to an impact assessment. In addition to vague goals, the means for reaching the goals are unclear. "Innovation" is not a method but a way of classifying all interventions by their degree of novelty. And because anything new is an innovation, the health education program may encourage the temporary adoption of a wide variety of techniques likely to vary widely from site to site. In short, it must be clear what the intended intervention is.

Third, a program's impact may be estimated only if it is possible to credibly approximate what would have happened to the targeted recipients in the absence of the program. (See our earlier discussion of causality.) For example, randomized experiments are a powerful means to make causal inferences about the impact of social programs, but, more generally, constructing comparison groups of various kinds, whether by random assignment or not, is usually essential. Hence, a program that is universal in its coverage and that has been going on for some period of time is very difficult (perhaps impossible) to evaluate for effectiveness. It is difficult to evaluate, therefore, the effectiveness of the current U.S. income tax system because there is no other income tax system for the country as a whole to which comparisons can be made. Comparisons to other countries or to much earlier historical periods raise very difficult questions of comparability. Serious problems of this sort plague ongoing attempts to estimate the effects of recent reforms to public welfare because the new legislation applies to all states, and it is very difficult to identify what would have happened if the reforms did not occur (Besharov, Germanis, and Rossi 1997).

To illustrate further the need for comparisons, a county in Northern California wanted an impact assessment of prosecutorial efforts to increase the likelihood that serious drug offenders would be sanctioned severely and swiftly. One of the evaluation outcomes was citizens' fear of crime; presumably, swift and severe sanctions would bring down the crime rate, at least for drug-related offenses, thereby lowering citizens' apprehensions about crime. Unfortunately, the evaluation was requested after the program began, and no measurement of citizens' attitudes before the start of the program was possible. Without such a pretest, it is simply impossible to tell whether the program made any difference. As a result, the plan to evaluate the program's impact on fear of crime was essentially abandoned.

Finally, effectiveness evaluations are often the most difficult kinds of evaluations, requiring highly trained personnel and, sometimes, large sums of money. Thus, it is silly to plan evaluations of program impact unless there are sufficient resources and unless appropriately trained professionals are available. Unfortunately, legislatures and administrators have often mistakenly required effectiveness evaluations from agencies that are not prepared to undertake them, often assuming as well that the costs would be modest (Raizen and Rossi 1981). For example, federal legislation has in the past required the National Institute of Justice to undertake an impact assessment of the large grants awarded to states and counties to "fight drugs." Yet, there was no accompanying appropriation and, at least informally, there were unrealistically high expectations about what could be learned.

There are no hard-and-fast rules about how much an effectiveness evaluation should cost or about how much skill may be needed to undertake it. However, sometimes a useful starting point for discussions of research costs is to ask that the equivalent of at least 5 to 10% of the program's operating budget be available for program evaluation. For the requisite research skills, it is always helpful if the individuals who will be doing the evaluation have *successfully* done such research in the recent past; a track record is very important, far more important than formal credentials.

Techniques have been developed (Wholey 1977) to determine whether a program is evaluable in the senses discussed previously. Decision makers are well advised to commission such studies as a first step rather than to assume that all programs can be evaluated. Evaluability assessments essentially determine whether there are program goals that are sufficiently well articulated, whether the program is sufficiently clear and uniformly delivered, and whether the requisite resources are available.

Stage 5: Did the Program Work?
The Effectiveness Question

As discussed previously, any assessment of whether or not a program "worked" necessarily assumes that what the program was *supposed* to accomplish is known. For a variety of reasons, enabling legislation-establishing programs often appears to set relatively vague objectives for the program, making it necessary to develop specific goals during the design phase. Goals for such general programs may be devised by stakeholders through consideration of their own experience, social science theory, past research, advice from experts, or studies of the problem that the program is supposed to ameliorate. In whatever way goals may be established, the important point is that it is not possible to determine whether a program worked without developing a limited and specific set of criteria for establishing the condition of "having worked." Beyond clear goals, therefore, there needs to be a rather clear concept of "how good is good enough."

For example, it would not have been possible to develop an assessment of whether "Sesame Street" worked without having identified that its goals were to foster reading and number-handling skills. Once that was determined, there still remained the vital question of how large a gain in performance was to be called a "success." Learning half the alphabet? One fourth? The full alphabet and all ten numerals? In other words, without specificity about the size and direction of the program effect required, program evaluators are shooting at a moving target.

Without such specificity, there will also not be enough information about the effects being sought to properly inform a number of critical design decisions. For example, there will be no way to determine the necessary sample size because the appropriate sample size depends in part on the size of the effect one is trying to detect; in general, smaller anticipated effects require larger samples to detect them. Likewise, it will be very difficult to decide how to measure the outcome variable. Again, the amount of precision depends on the size of the effect being sought. For example, one may well lose the ability to calculate significance tests designed maximally to address whether the program worked as hoped (e.g., Goodman and Royall 1988). One could not, for instance, define the null hypothesis in terms of the amount of effectiveness required for the program to be called a success.

It is important to note that program inventors and managers typically exaggerate the expected effects of their programs, interpretable as wishful thinking born out of zeal and commitment. It is unwise to design an impact assessment on the basis of advocates' expectations because that might lead to a research design that is not powerful enough to detect real but much smaller actual effects.

Finally, the evaluation report will be subject to a large number of ad hoc interpretations because the definition of success will often be person-specific. One person's success may be another person's failure. That is, two individuals examining the same empirical results may legitimately draw contradictory conclusions. Assuming, however, that "success" is properly defined, one must still respond to the reality that programs never succeed or fail in absolute terms. Success or failure is always relative to some benchmark. Hence an answer to the question, "Did the program work?" requires consideration of the question, "Compared to what?"

The "compared to what?" question is by now an old friend, introduced most thoroughly when we earlier considered impact assessment of new programs. Recall that impact assessments for new programs were generally best undertaken with randomized experiments. By and large, randomized designs are still the method of choice, although for ongoing social programs, random assignment faces a number of additional practical obstacles. For example, program recipients may feel entitled to a service they have been receiving for some time. Consider, for instance, the availability of unmetered water in a number of rural communities. The switch to metered water would generate a public outcry (and has in some locales), perhaps especially if coupled with random assignment. Access to water from local aquifers, rivers, streams, and lakes is, in many areas, part of the rights that historically have come with ownership of land.

In short, it is time to briefly review alternatives to randomized experiments; we must allow for the possibility that comparisons to the intervention may involve nonrandomly constructed groups of various kinds. Note, in addition, that although the alternatives are likely to be especially relevant to impact assessments of ongoing programs, they may also be used (as a second choice) in impact assessments of new programs.

The development of appropriate comparisons can proceed along at least three dimensions: (a) comparisons across different participants, (b) comparisons across different settings, and (c) comparisons across different times. In the first instance, one might compare different sets of persons, trying to hold constant the setting and when the study is undertaken. In the second instance, one might compare the performance of the same set of persons in different settings, such as at home and at work (necessarily at two different points in time). In the third instance, one might compare the same participants in the same setting but at different points in time.

Consider as an example different levels of aggregation involved in school settings (individual students, classes, and schools) and the time structuring of schooling (class periods, terms, and academic years). As Table 4.1 indicates, it is possible to mix these three fundamental dimensions to develop a wide variety of comparison groups. For example, comparison group C_2 varies both the participants and the setting, although the time is the same. Or comparison group C_6 varies the participants, the setting, and the time. However, with each added dimension by which one or more comparison groups differ from the experimental group, the number of threats to the validity of the resulting effectiveness estimates necessarily increases. For example, the use of comparison group C_4 (different setting and different time period) requires that assessment of program impact simultaneously take into account possible confounding factors associated with the reactive potential of different classroom environments and learning that has occurred over time.

As an illustration of the difficulties that often follow in the absence of random assignment, consider the evaluation (Robertson 1980) of the effectiveness of high school driver education programs in which the goal was to reduce automobile accidents among 16- to 18-year-olds. Despite sympathy for the programs, the state legislature decided not to provide any funding. In response, some school districts dropped

TABLE 4.1.   A Typology of Comparison Groups

	Same Subjects		Different Subjects	
	Same Setting	Different Setting	Same Setting	Different Setting
Same Time	XX[a]	XX[b]	C_1	C_2
Different Time	C_3	C_4	C_5	C_6

a. No comparison is possible.
b. Although logically possible, it is not feasible in practice.

driver education from their high school curriculum and some retained it.

Two sets of comparisons were possible: (a) accident rates for persons of the appropriate age range in the districts that dropped the program computed before and after the program was dropped, and (b) accident rates for the same age groups in the districts that retained driver education compared with the accident rates in districts that dropped the driver education program. It was found that the accident rates were significantly lower in those districts that dropped the program, a finding that might lead one to believe that the program *increased* the risk of accidents, perhaps because young people were enticed to obtain licenses earlier. However, internal validity in this instance depends on considerable knowledge about the process by which some school boards dropped the program. In most cases, school boards apparently dropped the program because of financial considerations. If (and only if) one can accept that local financial concerns were unrelated to the number of automobile accidents in the past, can the (unfortunate) inferences about the impact of the driver education program be taken seriously.

Of course, randomization will, on the average, eliminate confounding influences in the estimation of impact. On grounds of analytic simplicity alone, it is easy to see why so many expositions of impact assessment strongly favor research designs based on random assignment. As noted earlier, however, random assignment is often impractical or even impossible. Even when random assignment is feasible, its advantages rest on randomly assigning a relatively large number of participants. To randomly assign only two schools to the experimental group and only two schools to the control group, for example, will not allow the average equivalence between experimentals and controls to materialize. In an evaluation of a school-based program to change the nutrition habits of schoolchildren through instruction in nutrition and by changes in school meals, it was necessary to randomize close to 100 elementary schools in order to achieve the appropriate level of statistical power (Luepker et al. in press).

It is sometimes possible either to solve or to partially bypass comparison group problems by resorting to some set of external criteria as a baseline. For example, it is common in studies of desegregation or affirmative action programs to apply various measures of equity as a comparison group (Baldus and Cole 1977). In jury composition litigation, for instance, the baseline representation of Hispanics may be taken to be their representation on voter registration lists. If the proportion of Hispanics in the jury pool is lower than their proportion on voter registration lists, there is evidence of a potential problem.

Sometimes an external baseline is used to clarify possible comparisons. Thus, an assessment of whether schools in Black neighborhoods are being funded at comparable levels to schools in White neighborhoods might apply the criterion that disparities in excess of ±5% in expenditures per pupil indicate inequality (Berk and Hartman 1972). However, the use of such external baselines by themselves still leaves open the question of causal inference. It may be difficult to determine if the program or some other set of factors produced the observed relationship between outcomes of interest and the external metric. For example, the lower funding of schools in Black neighborhoods may stem from discriminatory policies of the school board or the greater seniority—and higher salaries—of teachers working in the schools of White neighborhoods.

To summarize, although comparisons are essential for estimating program effectiveness, and although randomized experiments are usually the most desirable research design for that purpose, one is often faced with the need to conduct impact assessments using comparisons not subject to random assignment. To that end, there are a wide variety of quasi-experimental designs that can be instructive, especially when the data they produce are properly analyzed. We turn now to a brief discussion of some key quasi-experimental designs and will later consider broadly what a good data analysis entails.

TABLE 4.2. A Typology of Research Designs

Research Design Type	Assignment Mechanism	Treatment Effects
I. Randomized ("true") Experiments	Known-stochastic	$\bar{Y}_E - \bar{Y}_C$
II. Regression-discontinuity	Known-deterministic	$(\bar{Y}_E \mid A) - (\bar{Y}_C \mid A)$
III. Interrupted time series	Unknown-hypothesized	$(\bar{Y}_{t2} \mid T, V) - (\bar{Y}_{t1} \mid T, V)$
IV. Cross-section	Unknown-hypothesized	$(\bar{Y}_E \mid X) - (\bar{Y}_C \mid X)$
V. Polled cross-section time series (panel)	Unknown-hypothesized	$(\bar{Y}_{E,\, t2} \mid T, V, X) -$ $(\bar{Y}_{C,\, \bar{Y}_E,\, t1} \mid T, V, X)$

NOTE: $\bar{Y}$ = "average" outcome; E = experimental group; C = comparison group; A = assignment variable(s); t_1 = before the intervention; t_2 = after the intervention; X = confounded variables covariates; T = trends; and V = events.

Some Research Designs
for Estimating Effectiveness

The discussion of comparison group strategies in the past few pages has necessarily been couched in relatively abstract terms. The actual practice of choosing among such strategies leads to a large variety of research designs. A topology of research design types commonly used for assessing the effectiveness of programs is shown in Table 4.2.

There are two dimensions to the typology: (a) what is known about the mechanism by which some units (e.g., people) were exposed to the program and some units were exposed to the control condition, and (b) how an overall causal effect may be operationalized. Regarding knowledge of the assignment mechanism (middle column in Table 4.2), there are three possible situations.

First, the mechanism may be known, but the result (i.e., assignment to the experimental or control condition) cannot be known in advance. That is, the mechanism is stochastic. Flipping a coin is an illustration.

Second, the mechanism may be known, and it is possible to know the result in advance as well. That is, the mechanism is deterministic. Assigning solely on the basis of some observable characteristic such as income is an illustration; individuals with incomes below some threshold are given income subsidies, and individuals with income above some threshold are not given income subsidies.

Third, the assignment may be unknown but hypothesized. For example, there may be a number of factors determining which households adopt recycling practices and which do not. It may be impossible to know exactly what those factors are, but it is certainly possible to develop informed hypotheses.

Under the operationalization of causal effects, there are a number of different possibilities. The most important differences, however, depend on whether the causal effect is defined in terms of cross-sectional comparisons or longitudinal comparisons and on what additional information may be taken into account to make the comparison "fair." For example, we will see that for randomized experiments, the usual comparisons are cross-sectional, and fair comparisons require nothing more than knowing what intervention was received by each unit. Other designs are more complicated to analyze. In any case, for each design there are several ways to define an overall treatment effect (e.g., as a difference or a ratio). Those listed in the last column of Table 4.2 are among the most common and will suffice for expositional purposes.

Design Type I: Randomized ("True") Experiments

We begin our exposition of Table 4.2 by returning to randomized experiments. Although we have a few new points to make, our main goal is to provide a benchmark by which alternative designs may be judged.

The gold standard for internal validity requires random assignment to experimental and control groups. As we have observed a number of times, the essential feature of true experiments is the random assignment of the treatment to units and the random withholding of the treatment from units, constituting, respectively, an experimental and a control group. The mechanism by which the assignment occurs is, therefore, known. However, it is a chance mechanism, because there is no way of determining before the assignment which units will be experimentals and which will be controls. The uncertainty creates no problems, however, because, in effect, assignment results from a fair lottery, which on the average makes the units assigned to the experimental group the same as the units assigned to the control group. That is, all external confounding influences are eliminated; the groups are on the average comparable before the intervention is introduced. Hence, comparisons between the groups are legitimate.

True experiments have a number of other assets (Berk et al. 1985; Boruch 1997). Perhaps most important, appropriate estimates of average treatment impact can be obtained from a simple comparison between the average outcome for the experimentals and the average outcome for the controls. The comparison may be a difference (as shown in Table 4.2) or a ratio. And the "average" may be a mean, median, or any other sensible measure of central tendency. One might in an experiment on the impact of a job training program, for instance, use the difference in postintervention median income between the experimentals and controls.

As noted earlier, another important advantage of randomized experiments is that if they are properly implemented, the assumptions necessary for statistical inferences are likely to be met. In the random assignment process itself is found the justification for conventional statistical inference. One does not have to rely on large samples to justify statistical inference or on particular assumptions about how the outcome measures are distributed (e.g., normal).

Still, randomized experiments are not free of assumptions. Two additional assumptions must be made (Rubin 1986). First, the participants must not be affected by the assignment mechanism itself. Thus, if experimental participants or controls behave differently knowing that they were assigned at random than if they were assigned in some other way, one will obtain an inaccurate estimate of treatment impacts. For example, control participants in a job training evaluation may misinterpret the random placement as an indication that they have been judged less worthy. This, in turn, may undermine their self-confidence and ability to perform in the labor market.

Second, one must assume that intervention received by the experimentals has no impact on the controls, and vice versa. For example, suppose one wanted to test the impact of teaching mathematics in a new way to primary school students. If teachers in the control group are threatened by the new technology, they may just work harder within their conventional curriculum to show administrators that the new approach is unnecessary. This is sometimes called a John Henry Effect and can influence the responses of controls. One way to help ensure that such problems do not materialize is to offer the control participants a placebo that is indistinguishable from the experimental condition. For biomedical experiments this is both easy to do and common practice. For example, the real medicine in tablet form cannot be distinguished from mere sugar in tablet form. But for evaluations of social programs, finding credible placebos is typically very difficult.

If either assumption is substantially violated—that the assignment mechanism does not affect the outcome and that what one group receives does not affect the outcome of the other group—there are at least two complications. Clearly, treatment content has been altered, which makes any substantive interpretations of the results more difficult. In addition, a number of important properties of the data necessary for statistical inference no longer hold. For example, the outcomes for the experimentals and controls may be related (not independent).

Randomized experimentals can be undermined in other ways. Everything depends on the experiment being implemented as designed, and at least three kinds of serious problems can occur. Sometimes the random assignment is not implemented properly. This can happen if the process of random assignment is misunderstood or subverted (Berk and Sherman 1988). For example, in an experiment undertaken in Detroit on the deterrent impact of arresting shoplifters, individuals apprehended for shoplifting by department store security personnel were to be assigned at random to one of two conditions: (a) arrest and (b) reprimand and release. However, the assignment pattern was initially alternating: Odd-numbered cases received arrest and even-numbered cases received reprimand and release. As a result, store personnel were often able to anticipate the assignment outcome and some used this information to pair particular individuals with particular treatments. With perhaps the best of intentions, they were trying to make sure that accused shoplifters got "what they deserved." As a result, the experimental and control groups were no longer comparable before the treatment was introduced; it is likely that the experimental group overrepresented customers who were seen engaging in more serious acts of shoplifting. This, in turn, might have led to underestimates of the impact of apprehension.

A second kind of problem occurs when the study participants do not fully comply with the experimental and control protocols. For example, Bickman and his colleagues (1997) conducted a study in Stark County, Ohio, comparing the 6-month functional and symptom outcomes of children and adolescents with serious emotional disturbances who received services in an exemplary system of care with outcomes of children who received traditional care. In this randomized experiment, a key issue addressed in the analysis was whether the experimental participants were really getting the "exemplary" care they were supposed to get. They would not if they did not take advantage of the services offered. Thus, if experimental participants with especially serious symptoms were more likely to take advantage of the mental health services, the experimental group would have contained a more problematic mix of patients than the control group. This might have led to underestimates of the beneficial impact of the treatment. Fortunately, compliance did not turn out to be a problem.

Sometimes compliance issues are of necessity built into the design. For example, Rossi, Berk, and Lenihan (1980) tested whether the provision of unemployment compensation for inmates after release from prison would reduce the likelihood of rearrest for new crimes. However, they could only randomly assign the opportunity to receive unemployment compensation, because whether payments were made depended on whether former prisoners in the experimental group obtained employment: Those who earned wages from jobs they found after release were not entitled to payments. Sometimes such experiments are called *intent-to-treat* studies. Later we will briefly discuss how to properly analyze the data from randomized experiments in which compliance is a problem, whether by misfortune or design.

A third kind of problem stems from attrition by participants from the study after random assignment. Attrition before random assignment can affect external validity, but internal validity will be sound. Attrition after random assignment can affect both internal validity and external validity if the kinds of participants who are lost from the experimental group differ from those who are lost from the control group (i.e., differential attrition). When this occurs, the comparability of the experimental and control groups can be compromised. Continuing with Bickman's experiment on "exemplary" mental health care services in Stark County, Ohio (Bickman et al. 1997), another concern was differential attrition because a substantial percentage of participants (as much as 25%) did not complete follow-up questionnaires from which many of the key outcome measures were taken. If, for example, participants in the control group with less serious symptoms were less motivated to participate in the study (because they were getting the usual services anyway and were not that troubled to begin with), and if that led to high rates of attrition, the control group would have overrepresented more problematic cases. Estimates of the beneficial impacts of the treatment could then have been too optimistic.

However, here, too, there was good news; the same kinds of participants seemed to be lost from both the experimental and control
groups, so that comparability was maintained.

To summarize, like all empirical research, randomized experiments
rely on some assumptions that are often not directly testable. The
number of such assumptions, however, is far fewer than other research
designs require and can be kept to a minimum if random assignment
is properly implemented. One implication is that randomized experiments must be implemented with great care. Another is that straightforward interpretations do not necessarily follow from results of true
experiments: *Caveat emptor.*

Finally, we discuss some minor definitional issues. First, we have
used the term *control group* in the context of random assignment. We
will now use the term *comparison group* when there is no random
assignment. Although this convention is common, it is not universal.
Second, when there is more than one treatment condition and one
control condition, we speak of two or more treatments and, correspondingly, two or more treatment groups. Then, there is no control
group or comparison group as such.

Design Type II: Regression Discontinuity
(Assignment by Observed Variables)

Some programs are administered using a clear set of rules for
selecting participants. For example, some college fellowship programs
allocate fellowships on the basis of scores received on standardized
tests (e.g., the National Merit Scholarship Test). In a similar fashion,
eligibility for food stamps is determined by income. Likewise, access
to privileges in prison is often decided by the number of incurred
disciplinary infractions. Note that in all three illustrations there is, at
least in principle, a threshold that cleanly and definitively determines
whether benefits are provided. Individuals above (or below) the threshold
receive benefits, whereas individuals below (or above) the threshold
do not. That is, there is no uncertainty in the assignment process.

If such administrative rules are followed faithfully, it is possible to
obtain fair (unbiased) estimates of treatment effect if, in addition to
the assumptions required for randomized experiments, one additional
assumption is met. One must assume for the experimental group and
the comparison group the same functional form for the relationship

between the variable used to determine who gets support (e.g., test scores) and the outcome (e.g., grade point average in college). A linear form or simple polynomial is commonly used.

The reason for the additional assumption is easily understood. Recall that in the case of random assignment, the experimentals and controls were on the average comparable. When assignment is determined by some threshold on an observed variable such as a test score, however, there is good reason to suspect that the experimentals and comparisons are not comparable. In general, then, students with higher test scores may well perform better in college.

The solution is to use information about the relationship between the assignment variable and the outcome to infer how the comparison group would have performed if their values on the assignment variable were on the average the same as those of the experimental group. If, for example, the relationship between test scores and later grade point average is linear, one can easily extrapolate what the grade point averages of the comparison group would have been had they had test scores identical on the average to the experimental group. Then, these extrapolated values may be compared to the observed grade point averages of the experimentals. For example, one might compute the simple difference between the two. Unfortunately, if the functional form is wrong, the extrapolations will be wrong, and as a result, the comparison will be misleading.

In practice, there is often evidence in the data that may make one functional form more plausible than others. It cannot be overemphasized, however, that there will be no experimental and comparison group members with the same values on the assignment variable. As a consequence, there are no means to fully verify empirically that the assumed functional form is correct. Evidence for a particular extrapolation is a long way from proof that the extrapolation is accurate.

The argument just made is simply summarized in Table 4.2 in the column Treatment Effects. If one knows the assignment variable (or combination of variables) and how it was used (i.e., the threshold), one may obtain unbiased estimates of the treatment effect after controlling (via statistical procedures such as analysis of covariance; more on that later) for the assignment variable. That is, the treatment effect is conditional on values of the assignment variable ("A"). It is in this process of making statistical adjustments that a functional form must be assumed, and one is essentially looking for a discontinuity (or "jump") in the estimated regression line based on that functional form, hence the term *regression discontinuity design*. The regression discontinuity design is, for some, counterintuitive. Apparently, it is hard to believe that after controlling for the assignment variable (and only the assignment variable), the experimental and comparison groups are on the average comparable. But the assignment variable is the sole vehicle by which assignment was undertaken, and how it was used is known exactly for each unit. In a manner analogous to random assignment, controlling for the assignment variable, therefore, severs all relationships between variables related to the outcome and the intervention assigned. Unbiased estimates follow.

Regression discontinuity designs are particularly useful when programs assign benefits on the basis of some measured variable. With no extra effort, a powerful quasi-experimental design is already in place (e.g., Berk and Rauma 1983). In addition, regression discontinuity designs are sometimes useful alternatives to true experiments when random assignment is politically or ethically unacceptable. One may assign on the basis of "need" or any other attribute as long as there is an observable variable on which a threshold may be placed (for more details, see Trochim 1984). Berk and de Leeuw (1997) have formally extended regression discontinuity designs to evaluations in which the outcome is binary (e.g., pass or fail), or a count (e.g., number of arrests), or to situations in which the treatments are analogous to dose levels (e.g., differing weeks of job training), rather than discrete conditions. Thus, regression discontinuity designs now have much of the same formal generality as randomized experiments.

Design III: Interrupted Time Series

Interrupted time-series designs are based on repeated measures, over time, of some outcome. Simply put, the idea is to compare the time trend before an intervention with the time trend after. For example, a downward trend in the conviction rate for a particular jurisdiction may be reversed after more prosecutors are hired. Or air pollution levels downwind from a major power plant may be relatively stable over several years until a dramatic drop materializes following the introduction of cleaner burning fuels.

Time-series analyses are especially important for estimating the net impacts of full coverage programs. Under full coverage, all the units that could be served are being served. As a consequence, there are no reasonable comparison groups. However, if a relatively large number of observations are collected before and after the intervention, the earlier period provides a comparison group for the later period. Thus, it may be possible to study the effect of the enactment of a gun control law in a particular jurisdiction, but only if the evaluator has access to a sufficiently lengthy series of crime statistics for gun-related offenses, both before and after the law was enacted. Or the effects of changing pricing policies on residential water consumption can be studied by analyzing the consumption trends, if consumption data can be found before and after the pricing policy changes (Berk et al. 1981). Of course, for many interventions such long-term measures do not exist. For example, there are no long-term, detailed time series on the incidence of certain acute diseases, making it difficult to assess the impact on those diseases of the enactment of Medicare or Medicaid.

The basic logic underlying the analysis or interrupted time-series designs is quite simple. The time series before the intervention is analyzed so that temporal trends (or patterns) before the intervention are characterized as accurately as possible. For example, the number of burglaries may be increasing at an alarming rate. Then the preintervention trends are used to project what would have happened without the intervention. Finally, the observed trends after the intervention are compared with the projections. In its simplest form, the preintervention mean is compared to the postintervention mean, as shown in Table 4.2 (where "T" stands for trends and "V" stands for events).

Although capturing the preintervention trends is a necessary condition for accurate estimates of treatment impact, it is not sufficient. One must also take into account events, in addition to the intervention, that are related to when the intervention was introduced and could affect postintervention trends. For example, a reduction in water consumption after an increase in the marginal price might be obscured by an overall increase in water consumption because of a major leak in the water distribution system. Or an apparent reduction in water consumption after an increase in the marginal price may really result from the installation of new water-saving irrigation technology that was purchased well before the price increase was even contemplated.

In other words, one must take into account events whose effects may be confounded with the intervention. The key idea is that events occurring about the same time as the intervention must be addressed. Put in the terms we used previously, the assignment process is one of timing. All units receive the intervention because there is only one unit: a company, a household, a city, a school district, or even a single individual (Kadzin 1982). What needs to be addressed is not which units receive the intervention and which do not, but *when* the intervention is introduced. It is this assignment process that must be considered, and all variables related to the timing of the intervention, which also may affect the postintervention trends, must be taken into account. We show this in Table 4.2 by including as conditioning variables not only time trends (T) but confounding events (V). In practice, the Vs are "taken into account" with multivariate statistical techniques that are beyond the scope of this book.

The most serious limitation on time-series designs is the need to properly adjust, in the statistical analysis, for preexisting trends (T) and events that are roughly contemporaneous with the intervention (V). These trends cannot be known with the same confidence that the assignment mechanism can be known for either the randomized experiment or the regression discontinuity design. They must be hypothesized, capitalizing on theory, past research, and information in the data on hand. And there is ultimately no way to directly test whether the Ts and Vs taken into account are the full set of Ts and Vs that should have been taken into account. Put another way, in addition to all of the assumptions required for randomized experiments, one must accurately hypothesize what Ts and Vs are relevant and, typically, the functional forms of their relationships with the outcome.

Another obstacle is that the number of preintervention and postintervention observations must be sufficient to reveal accurately preintervention and postintervention time trends (more than 25 observations for each are sometimes recommended). For this reason, interrupted time-series designs are often restricted to outcomes for which governmental or other groups routinely collect and publish the needed statistics. Despite these and other drawbacks, however, the interrupted time-series design can be very effective when more powerful designs are not available. They are especially useful when the units studied are large, such as neighborhoods, businesses, or cities. One recent example is an evaluation of Houston's community policing efforts (Kessler and Duncan 1996) in which changes in the number of crimes over time were studied as a function of changing policing practices.

Design Type IV: Cross-Sectional Designs

Whereas interrupted time-series designs were characterized by temporal variation only, cross-sectional designs are characterized by cross-sectional variation only. One is simply examining whether two or more sets of units differ at some specific moment in time. One set, for example, might be cities that earlier passed rent-control ordinances and another set might be cities that did not. Then the central empirical comparison might be between the current median vacancy rates for similar kinds of apartments in the two kinds of cities: the median vacancy rate for rent-controlled cities versus the median vacancy rate for non-rent-control cities. That is, the outcome is measured at only one moment in time and only as a posttest. Hence, comparisons can only be between units at that historical moment.

Much as in randomized experiments and regression discontinuity designs, one is interested in a comparison of units exposed to the intervention with units not exposed to the intervention. However, unlike true experiments and regression discontinuity designs, the assignment mechanism must be hypothesized. And if the hypothesized assignment mechanism is not effectively the same as the true assignment mechanism, the comparisons between the exposed and unexposed units will lead to misleading treatment-effect estimates. Stated a bit differently, the problem is that members of the exposed and unexposed groups are not likely to be on the average comparable before the intervention is introduced. Insofar as these differences are also related to the outcome measure, the effect of preexisting differences between the experimental and comparison groups will be confounded with the treatment effect. The only hope, then, is to make the groups conditionally comparable by controlling for the variables determining assignment. We show this in Table 4.2 by making the treatment effect conditional on X.

Consider, for example, a program to make judges more sensitive to the special nature of domestic violence cases. Judges are offered weekend workshops in which they learn about the nature of domestic violence and the special needs of both victims and offenders. As a result of these workshops, sentencing patterns are supposed to change. Now suppose that the potential change in sentencing patterns is being estimated by comparing the sentences given by judges who participate in the workshops with the sentences given by judges who do not (i.e., a cross-sectional comparison). For expositional purposes, assume that judges are simply encouraged to volunteer for the weekend workshops. Clearly, not all judges would participate, and those who did might well differ from those who did not. For example, judges already concerned about the issues might well be the ones more likely to volunteer. And these judges might already sentence differently. Alternatively, they might be individuals who would have changed their sentencing practices anyway in the near future. How, then, can a fair comparison be made?

For simplicity, suppose that "concern about domestic violence" is the only factor affecting the likelihood that judges would volunteer for the workshops. Clearly, if for each experimental-group judge a comparison-group judge could be found who was equally "concerned," the two groups would be matched on the selection variable on which participation depended. The two groups would then be comparable person by person.

Exact matching is often impractical because no exact, or even approximate, matches can be found. Therefore, as an alternative, statistical adjustments are often undertaken that equate the experimental and comparison groups on the average. That is, the central tendencies (usually means) of the two groups are equated on factors that differ before the intervention is introduced; the two groups are made comparable on the average. In this illustration, the group of judges who did not volunteer would have the same average level of concern about domestic violence as the group of judges who did volunteer. With these adjustments made, the groups can be fairly compared.

In practice, the necessary adjustments are not easily made. In addition to all of the assumptions required in randomized experiments, one must assume that *all* of the variables affecting assignment and the outcome are known and measured. These variables should be chosen by developing a selection model for how units are assigned to the experimental and comparison conditions. But because such a model is only hypothesized, internal validity is always in jeopardy.

That is, there is no direct way to empirically validate the hypothesized selection model. Still, it is often possible to complete strong impact assessments with sufficient care and resources. An interesting illustration is a recent evaluation of counseling for Australian Vietnam War veterans who suffered from a variety of combat-related psychological problems (Dobson et al. 1996). Veterans who self-selected into counseling were compared to veterans who did not, with comparability addressed through statistical adjustments.

Design Type V: Pooled Cross-Sectional and Time-Series Designs (Panels)

Randomized experiments and regression discontinuity designs may rely on cross-sectional (across units) and time-series (over time) information. Cross-sectional comparisons are made between units who are exposed to the intervention and those who are not. But statistical power may be improved by including measures of the outcome variable *before* the intervention. That is, although preintervention measures of the outcome variable are not needed for unbiased treatment effect estimates, pretest measures allow one to more easily separate "real" treatment effects from "noise." Thus, true experiments and regression discontinuity designs may capitalize on longitudinal comparisons.

Under pooled cross-sectional and time-series designs (also known as "panel" designs), both cross-sectional and longitudinal comparisons may be made. However, we include under this heading only those situations in which the assignment mechanism is unknown. That is, just as in interrupted time-series and cross-sectional designs, the assignment mechanism must be hypothesized.

Consider, for example, whether a new drug slows the progression to AIDS among those people infected with HIV, the AIDS retrovirus (Pinkerton and Abramson 1996). The drug is made available to physicians to prescribe as they see fit, with the constraint that only one prescription for a week of treatment is permitted per patient. Now imagine a research design in which monthly data are collected for several years on a sample of HIV-infected individuals. That is, there is a monthly time series for each individual. Assume that the outcome measure is the T-cell count; the lower the count, the more compromised the immune system. The drug is the intervention. For those who take the new drug, the prescription's date is recorded. In addition, information is collected on a number of physical and behavioral variables potentially related to *both* the taking of the drug and the conversion to AIDS: other drugs being taken, other illnesses, sexual behavior, the use of "recreational drugs," diet, exercise, and the like. For example, an infected individual who feels he is eating well and getting sufficient exercise may be less likely to see a physician and also less likely to progress. Or an infected individual who engages in high-risk behavior, such as intravenous drug use, may be more likely to see a physician (as a precaution) and more likely to progress.

The analysis of the drug data may be seen initially as a set of interrupted time-series analyses, one for each individual who took the new drug. As before, one can compare time trends before taking the drug with time trends after, and potentially confounding events, such as contracting another illness, would need to be taken into account. Just as in an interrupted time-series design, the simplest analysis would contrast the mean (or median) T-cell count before the intervention with the mean (or median) T-cell count after the intervention. In addition, however, comparisons can be made across individuals between those who took the new drug and those who did not, much as in purely cross-sectional designs. Just as in purely cross-sectional designs, all variables affecting treatment assignment (i.e., taking the new drug) and the outcome (i.e., T-cell count) would need to be known, measured, and used in any analysis of the data. In the simplest analysis, the conditional mean for the individuals who took the drug would be compared with the conditional mean for the individuals who did not take the drug.

But it is possible to do better than either the longitudinal or cross-sectional analyses alone. One can effectively combine the two to address both confounding temporal variables and confounding cross-sectional variables. Again focusing on perhaps the simplest analysis, the mean T-cell count for the "nontreated" individuals would include the T-cell counts for individuals who were not treated at all and the T-cell counts during the preintervention period for individuals who ultimately were treated. The mean T-cell count for the treated individuals would include the T-cell counts for people who took the new drug in the postintervention period. And both means would be adjusted for (i.e., would be conditional on) trends (T), roughly contemporaneous events (V), and assignment variables (X). That is, one would adjust for both temporal and cross-sectional confounders.

Because pooled cross-sectional and time-series designs typically involve more data collection than either cross-sectional or interrupted time designs alone, one might wonder when they are worth the effort. In general, they should be undertaken when resources allow, assuming that true experiments and regression discontinuity designs are not practical. First, thinking of this in terms of many interrupted time series, the prospects for external validity are better than for a single interrupted time series. In our AIDS example, it is possible to explore how well the drug works for a large group of people, some of whom presumably vary in important ways.

Second, thought of as a set of cross-sectional comparisons arrayed over time, the prospects for external validity are better than for a single-point-in-time cross-sectional comparison. Again using our AIDS example, it is possible to explore how effective the drug is depending on when in the progression of the illness it is taken.

Third, the longitudinal and cross-sectional variations allow for both longitudinal and cross-sectional threats to internal validity to be addressed, at least in principle. In the AIDS illustration, one can adjust, for example, for time trends in the T-cell count (e.g., cycles during a downward trend), the confounding effect of earlier illnesses (e.g., herpes), and the confounding effect of age differences across infected individuals.

Pooled cross-sectional and time-series designs are common in evaluation research. A recent example is the Fort Bragg evaluation (Bickman et al. 1995) we have cited several times earlier. Patients, some exposed to managed mental health care and some not, were followed over time, and their psychological functioning was monitored. An earlier example is the study by Berk and his colleagues (1981) in which water consumption in a set of communities was measured for a number of months to determine how well different water programs worked.

A Few Words About Data Analysis
for Impact Assessments

Perhaps the key to internal validity for each of the designs just addressed is the way in which units wind up in the different treatment groups. A properly implemented randomized experimental solves this selection problem by employing a known chance mechanism. A properly implemented regression-discontinuity design solves this selection problem by employing a known deterministic mechanism. Thus, in both cases it is relatively easy to represent properly the selection process in the data analysis. For randomized experiments, simple comparisons between average outcomes will often suffice. For regression-discontinuity designs, simple comparisons between average outcomes will often suffice, after conditioning on the assignment variable(s). This is typically done by regression analysis of some sort, in which the outcome is treated as a function of the assignment variable(s) and the treatment variable(s). No other explanatory variables need be taken into account.

For all of the other designs, selection is far more problematic; the selection mechanism is *not* known but must be hypothesized. The key question for any data analysis, therefore, is how accurately the true (but unknown) selection mechanisms are represented. This question is probably addressed most directly by explicitly developing a statistical model of the selection. In effect, one makes the treatment or comparison group in which units are placed the outcome variable, taken to be a function of variables thought to affect which units wind up in which groups. For example, as an intermediate step in an evaluation of the impact of shelters, Berk and his colleagues (Berk, Newton, and Berk 1986) developed a model for which victims of spousal abuse were likely to seek refuge in a shelter. Among the explanatory variables were whether the victim had gone to a shelter before and whether the victim and offender were currently living together. Both were thought to increase the likelihood that a victim would seek refuge in a shelter.

How is a selection model used? Perhaps most powerfully, the selection model is used to generate the estimated probability for each unit of being included in each of the treatment groups. These "predicted probabilities" are then used as conditioning variables in any later analyses of program impact. The conditioning may be undertaken by matching or by multivariate statistical analysis, but it has been shown that matching by these predicted probabilities alone will make the experimental and comparison groups comparable on the average (assuming that the selection model is accurate). The predicted probabilities are often called *propensity scores,* and they have been increasingly used in what statisticians have called *observational studies* since their development by Donald Rubin and Paul Rosenbaum (Rosenbaum 1995). In the study of shelter impact just cited (Berk et al. 1986), the predicted probability of seeking refuge in a shelter was used as a control variable in a multivariate analysis when the impact of shelters was addressed. In effect, statistical adjustments were made for the tendency of women to seek refuge in shelters.

It is important to appreciate that the use of propensity scores does *not* guarantee strong internal validity. Far from it. Everything usually depends on the quality of the selection model. If the model is weak, internal validity will be weak as well. However, one advantage of using propensity scores is that it is often easier to apply a range of diagnostic procedures. For example, because propensity scores can be used as the single conditioning variable, simple scatterplots can be very instructive. Thus, Berk and Newton (1985) were able to plot separately for the experimental and comparison groups the relationship between propensity scores and the outcome in an evaluation of different police procedures in wife battery incidents. They found that the likelihood of new violence was greater in households in which the police did not arrest the offender and that this effect was especially pronounced for offenders whom the police would normally be most inclined to arrest. That is, the police were using arrest effectively, especially when high-risk offenders were singled out. Berk and Newton were also able to show that the scatterplot was consistent with the assumed linear relationship between the propensity scores and the outcome. That is, a very simple graph helped to justify the statistical model applied.

Partly in response to such concerns about the quality of the selection model, there has been interest of late in the development of sensitivity tests for the results from observational studies (Rosenbaum 1995). The basic idea is to try different models of the selection process and see under what circumstances the evaluation results change. In an ideal situation, the results will not change materially under a wide variety of plausible selection models. One then may be able to conclude that in an important sense, the potential bias in the selection process can be safely ignored. One may say that the evaluation results are "robust."

Another response has been the development of statistical procedures that under some circumstances can explicitly circumvent selection biases. These procedures are applications of "instrumental variable" techniques long used by econometricians (Arngrist et al. 1996; Bowden and Turkington 1984). In the ideal case, one has a "degraded" randomized experiment; units are assigned at random as usual, but the units do not necessarily receive the treatments they are supposed to. Recall the study by Rossi et al. (1980) in which prison inmates were randomly assigned to unemployment compensation eligibility. Whether or not an inmate actually received compensation depended on earnings in the labor force, which were not under experimental control. An instrumental variable approach would entail constructing a propensity score as a function of the random assignment and then using that variable to represent assignment to experimental and control groups. This situation is ideal because if the random assignment is free of selection bias (which it is, in principle), and if the propensity score is constructed from the random assignment indicator, then the propensity score also will be free of selection bias. In effect, Rossi et al. proceeded in this manner for parts of their analysis.

A more recent illustration can be found in an evaluation of the impact of mandatory remedial education that was part of a welfare reform experiment (GAIN) in California. The evaluation question was whether mandatory education improved the performance of former AFDC recipients on standardized tests measuring basic cognitive skills relevant to performance in the job market. In the experiment, remedial education was required for members of the experimental group, *who were deemed educationally deficient.* That is, the educational component was available for only a subset of the experimental group, and the subset within the experimental group was not determined by random assignment. Boudett and Friedlander (1997) constructed an instrumental variable for participation in mandatory education, in part as a function of the group to which participants were randomly assigned. Then the instrumental variable was used to estimate treatment effects.

The more common alternative to the construction and use of propensity scores is to adjust directly for average differences between experimental and comparison groups that may be related to the outcome. There is no concern with *why* the experimental and comparison groups are not on the average comparable before the treatment is introduced. The focus is solely on adjusting for those preexisting differences. As we noted earlier, matching or multivariate procedures such as least-squares regression can be used for this purpose. The key, however, is that all of the relevant preexisting differences are known, measured, and then included in the analysis. Recall that at best this will be a matter of degree, not fully subject to empirical test.

There also exist a large number of very elaborate statistical procedures, falling under the rubric of structural equation modeling (SEM), that can in principle more fully capture selection effects and treatment effects simultaneously. Sometimes SEM can also represent certain kinds of measurement error. (See our discussion of measurement in Chapter 2, this volume.) One can think of SEM as an extension of simpler regression procedures, and just as for regression, they require a number of assumptions that are difficult to meet in practice. For example, it is essential that measures of all confounding influences be included in a formal model of the program's impact, that their mathematical relationship to the outcome be properly specified (e.g., a linear additive form versus a multiplicative form), and that measurement error be accurately modeled. Should any of these requirements be violated, one risks serious bias in any estimates of program impact. There is a growing consensus among statisticians that data analysts have routinely pushed SEM procedures beyond where they were designed to go. (See, for example, Freedman 1987.) SEM has far too often been applied to data that are not even remotely appropriate, relying on assumptions that have virtually no justification. At this juncture, perhaps the best advice is that fancy statistical analyses are no substitute for random assignment, and statistical analyses should be simple and as close to the data as possible. Then it is vital to employ whatever diagnostic tools are available to refine the analysis and address how robust the findings really are.

When Should the Different Research Designs Be Used?

The number of different research designs is large. How can one choose between them? First, in any concrete situation, some research designs will be immediately eliminated because of cost, politics, ethics, or practical constraints. One can then choose from among the designs remaining. An instructive illustration is evaluations of programs for large units such as communities. For example, Treno and Holder (1997) considered efforts to reduce alcohol-involved death and injuries in three communities. Among the interventions were methods to assist alcoholic beverage servers and retail liquor establishments in reducing the likelihood that customers would become intoxicated, or drive when intoxicated, and in reducing the likelihood that underage customers would be served. Clearly, with but three units, random assignment makes little sense. Just as clearly, deterministic assignment makes little sense. However, an interrupted time-series design implemented in each of the three communities could be instructive, using alcohol-related automobile accidents as one outcome measure.

Second, among the set of designs that may be feasible, one should be chosen that provides the most credible results when all four kinds of validity are considered. Although we have stressed internal validity over the past few pages, it is but one of four considerations. This is not to say that all four kinds of validity should be treated equally. Particular circumstances will usually suggest that some kinds of validity are more important than others. As we have said many times, if internal validity dominates, then one should try to employ randomized experiments.

Third, one cannot ignore cost. As we noted earlier, the value of the information produced relative to the costs of the evaluation must be addressed. If there are not other considerations, the less expensive design is clearly preferable.

Fourth, one must not lose sight of how easy it will be to implement the design. The YOAA problem applies not just to programs but to evaluations. One implication is that an elegant research design that cannot be properly implemented can become an embarrassment for all. Thus, for example, we favor very simple randomized experiments that do not require complex calculations to determine assignment to experimental and control conditions (Berk and Sherman 1988). Another implication is that the evaluator must think through precisely how the design will be implemented and participate as much as possible to make that happen. In other words, the evaluator must be one part scientist and one part administrator. Just as in programs themselves, the nuts and bolts really matter. Offering up a fancy research design and then walking away until the data are ready for analysis is to risk having no data worthy of the name.

Fifth, the choice of which design to employ cannot be done by recipe. Although expertise and experience are very important, there will usually be a role for judgment calls. This means that the evaluator is often open to post hoc criticism about the design, and it will typically be useful to have as many stakeholders as possible sign off on the design before it is fielded.

Stage 6: Was the Program Worth It? The Cost-Effectiveness Question

In the previous chapter, the issue of cost-effectiveness was addressed. We have little to add because the issues for new programs and ongoing programs are much the same. Perhaps the major difference is that for ongoing programs, there is often more information about the long term to take into account. For example, insofar as staff salaries are tied to seniority, ongoing programs may become more expensive in constant dollars as their staffs age. For a new program, there is very little information about these kinds of processes that unfold over the long haul. In a similar fashion, there will be more information about benefits. The long-term returns to job training, for example, may be estimable from data rather than hypothesized from theory or extrapolated from past research. Given the central role of discounting, having data on such long-term costs and benefits can be very useful.

Stage 7: Putting the Findings in a Larger Context

When we earlier addressed external validity, we stressed that stakeholders rarely care only about the program being evaluated. They are typically interested in the bigger picture: what this evaluation says about programs of particular kinds, delivered to particular kinds of units, in particular kinds of settings, and particular kinds of time periods. Thus, the evaluation findings have to be placed in a larger context in order for their full import to be appreciated.

Sometimes this is best done by a conventional literature review in which a wide range of potentially relevant material is synthesized. Such reviews are by and large qualitative, although some report an informal "vote count" to summarize the results. One risk is that a number of implicit decisions are made in the process that are not precisely articulated and are, therefore, not open to external scrutiny.

For example, it is typically unclear how the methodological quality of different studies is weighted as the overall synthesis is constructed. In any case, a good evaluation will explain how the study at hand fits into this larger picture and what then may be concluded overall.

Often, a more quantitative synthesis can be useful. The goal is to turn the traditional literature review into a data analysis in which a number of studies are quantitatively explored at the same time. Such work comes in two flavors.

First, it is sometimes possible to acquire the raw data from a set of relevant studies and perform a secondary analysis that also includes the data from the evaluation at hand. Data from the earlier studies may be literally pooled with data from the new study, or very precise prior information (in Bayesian language) from the earlier studies may be extracted and then formally built into an analysis of the new study. For example, Berk and his colleagues (1992) simultaneously analyzed data from four randomized experiments testing different methods by which police might reduce the incidence of wife battery. The goal was to combine the results from one site with the results from the other three in order to arrive at some overall conclusions. Did the treatments that worked in one community work in others? If not, what could be learned about why certain treatments were more or less likely to be effective where? When raw data sets can be obtained and pooled in this manner, the researcher has flexibility to proceed in the most effective manner and an ability to carefully examine the data from any anomalies. Analyses with data from a number of studies can be a lot of work, but can lead to very powerful conclusions.

Sometimes the raw data for the set of relevant studies cannot be obtained or there are so many studies that the pooling approach is not practical. Then the second quantitative option is to conduct what is called a meta-analysis (Cook et al. 1992; Glass et al. 1981; Hedges and Olkin 1988). The basic goal in the ideal situation is to (a) canvass the population of relevant studies; (b) eliminate those studies that are methodologically weak; (c) construct measures of treatment effect size that can be used across all of the remaining studies; (d) compute summary measures of effect size over all of the studies, inversely weighting for the uncertainty in each study; and (e) report these summary measures along with confidence intervals. Often one can go further by reporting summary measures of treatment effects for different treatment variations, different sets of participants, different settings or times, and even different evaluation methods. Indeed, one can conduct multivariate analyses in which the size of the treatment effect is taken to be a function of just such factors. An instructive example is Lipsey's (1992) meta-analysis of juvenile delinquency treatment programs in which this kind of analysis was undertaken. He found, for instance, that employment-based interventions had the largest beneficial effects.

Although meta-analysis can be a very useful tool and certainly has its champions, our assessment is rather cautious. First, everything depends on the quality of the underlying studies. If they have weak validity overall, even the fanciest of meta-analyses cannot save the day. Meta-analysis cannot correct for fundamental flaws in the original research.

Second, because the raw data from these studies are not examined, methodological screening must rely on secondary accounts of the design, its implementation, and data quality. These can be very incomplete and even wrong. Then the results rest on studies whose quality cannot be judged properly.

Third, the measures of treatment impact across different studies are essentially standardized scores. For example, one might compute the differences in the means for the experimentals and controls on the outcome, divided by the standard deviation of the outcome. Thus, treatment effects are no longer in their original metric, which means that very different kinds of outcomes can be combined. For instance, job training programs that measure whether a person got a job can be combined with job training programs that measure how long it took for a person to get a job. Although this has the benefit of allowing a large number of studies to be analyzed, much of the original interpretation may be lost. In the end, it can be very difficult to determine how big is big. Is an average treatment effect of 5 large or small? The proper answer is that it often depends on information that is masked in the standardized measure of effect.

Fourth, the assumptions made in meta-analysis so that statistical inference can be applied are sometimes difficult to justify. For example, evaluation studies are not probability samples of anything. Yet their results are often treated as if they were random draws from some known population.

In our view, meta-analysis is almost always helpful as a *process*. Its systematic nature means that evaluators are likely to learn a great deal as the meta-analysis is being conducted. Meta-analysis can also be useful when similar studies of very high known validity are combined with the goal of increasing statistical power. This can be important if the studies taken in isolation were based on samples too small to detect important treatment effects. We are less sanguine about attempts to explain variation in treatment effects using multivariate statistical procedures. A great deal must be assumed for the statistical procedures to play through.

To summarize, if one really wants estimates of treatment effects across a number of different evaluations, the best approach is to obtain all of the relevant data and do a pooled analysis. When this is not feasible, meta-analysis can be an instructive fallback position. However, we cannot overemphasize that meta-analysis cannot correct for fundamental flaws in the original evaluations. Indeed, it risks just papering them over.

Finally, the procedures we have just described that provide a larger context for a given evaluation clearly can be used as stand-alone activities or ways to inform an evaluation at its earliest stages. Indeed, as we noted earlier, waiting until the end to learn what else has been done is usually a serious error.

Some Afterthoughts

The field of evaluation research is scarcely out of its infancy. The first large-scale field experiments were initiated in the mid-1960s. Concern for large-scale national evaluations of social programs had its origins in the War on Poverty. The art of designing large-scale implementation and monitoring studies is still evolving rapidly. Concern with the scientific validity of qualitative research has just begun. As part of all this, the demand for sound program evaluations continues to grow. In this context, perhaps the best overall message is to keep evaluations as simple as possible. Simple programs will typically be hard enough to design and field. Simple research designs usually will be sufficiently demanding. And simple data analyses will likely tax the best evaluators available. Put another way, there is no such thing as a routine evaluation. Adding unnecessary complexity to the burden is to turn a promising opportunity into almost certain disaster.

Simplicity, however, is not enough. It is also important to think defensively as if Murphy's Law always applies. Evaluation research is often a minefield of day-to-day problems for which the proper preparation can make an enormous difference. For example, it is typically useful to get, in writing, all significant understandings between the evaluator and program administrators (e.g., the definition of a successful outcome). Even under the best of circumstances and with the best of intentions, organizational memories can be very short. Likewise, it is essential that quality control procedures be introduced for all facets of data collection: sampling, measurement, data entry, and the like. Indeed, it is often prudent to allocate as much as 20% of one's evaluation research budget to data quality control. And before diving into a fancy statistical analysis, it is essential to carefully inspect the data for errors of various sorts that will almost certainly be present. This means not just a search for isolated "outliers," but internal consistency checks for anomalous relationships among key variables.

Finally, there is no fixed recipe. Prescriptions for "successful" evaluations are, in practice, prescriptions for failure. The techniques that evaluators may bring to bear are only tools, and even the very best of tools does not ensure a worthy product. Just as for any craft, there is no substitute for intelligence, experience, perseverance, and a touch of whimsy.

Bibliography

Abt Associates. 1979. *Child Care Food Program*. Cambridge, MA: Author.

American Psychologist. 1997. 52(5):536–65.

Angrist, J. D., G. W. Imbens, and D. B. Rubin. 1996. "Identification of Causal Effects Using Instrumental Variables." *Journal of the American Statistical Association* 91(434):444–55.

Baldus, D. C. and J. W. L. Cole. 1977. "Quantitative Proof of Intentional Discrimination." *Evaluation Quarterly* 1(1):53–86.

Barnett, V. 1982. *Comparative Statistical Inference*. New York: John Wiley.

Barron, E. J. 1995. "Climate Models: How Reliable Are Their Predictions?" *Consequences: The Nature and Implications of Environmental Change* 1(3):17–27.

Becker, H. S. 1958. "Problems of Inference and Proof in Participant Studies." *American Sociological Review* 23(6):652–60.

Berk, R. A. 1988a. "Causal Inference for Sociological Data." In *Handbook of Sociology*, edited by N. Smelser. Beverly Hills, CA: Sage.

———. 1988b. "The Role of Subjectivity in Criminal Justice Classification and Prediction Methods." *Criminal Justice Ethics* 6(1):183–200.

———. 1990. "Thinking About Hate Motivated Crime." *Journal of Interpersonal Violence* 5(3):334–49.

Berk, R. A., P. R. Abramson, and P. Okami. 1995. "Sexual Activity as Told in Surveys." In *Sexual Nature, Sexual Culture*, edited by P. R. Abramson and S. Pinkerson. Chicago: University of Chicago Press.

Berk, R. A., R. Boruch, D. Chambers, P. Rossi, and A. Witte. 1985. "Social Policy Experimentation: A Position Paper." *Evaluation Review* 9(4):387–429.

Berk, R. A. and M. Brewer. 1978. "Feet of Clay in Hobnailed Boots: An Assessment of Statistical Inference in Applied Research." Pp. 90–214 in *Evaluation Studies Review Annual*, Vol. 3, edited by T. D. Cook. Beverly Hills, CA: Sage.

Berk, R. A., A. Campbell, R. Klap, and B. Western. 1992. "The Differential Deterrent Effects of an Arrest in Incidents of Domestic Violence: A Bayesian Analysis of Four Randomized Experiments." *American Sociological Review* 57(5):689–708.

Berk, R. A. and T. E. Cooley. 1987. "Errors in Forecasting Social Phenomena." *Climate Change* 11(2):247–65.

109

Berk, R. A., T. E. Cooley, C. J. LaCivita, and K. Sredl. 1981. *Water Shortage: Lessons in Water Conservation Learned From the Great California Drought.* Cambridge, MA: Abt Books.

Berk, R. A. and J. de Leeuw. 1997. *An Evaluation of a Inmates Placement System Using a Regression-Discontinuity Design.* Los Angeles: University of California, Los Angeles, Center for Statistics, Working Paper.

Berk, R. A. and D. A. Freedman. 1995. "Statistical Assumptions as Empirical Commitments." In *Law Punishment and Social Control: Essays in Honor of Sheldon Messinger,* edited by T. Blomberg and S. Cohen. New York: Adline de Gruyter.

Berk, R. A. and A. Hartman. 1972. "Race and Class Differences in Per Pupil Staffing Expenditures in Chicago Elementary Schools." *Integrated Education* 10(1):52–57.

Berk, R. A. and P. J. Newton. 1985. "Does Arrest Really Deter Wife Battery? An Effort to Replicate the Findings of the Minneapolis Spouse Abuse Experiment." *American Sociological Review* 50:253–62.

Berk, R. A., P. J. Newton, and S. F. Berk. 1986. "What a Difference a Day Makes: An Empirical Study of the Impact of Shelters for Battered Women." *Journal of Marriage and the Family* 48:481–90.

Berk, R. A. and D. Rauma. 1983. "Capitalizing on Nonrandom Assignment to Treatments: A Regression Discontinuity Evaluation of a Crime Control Program." *Journal of the American Statistical Association* 78:21–28.

Berk, R. A. and P. H. Rossi. 1976. "Doing Good or Worse: Evaluation Research Politically Reexamined." *Social Problems* 23(4):337–49.

Berk, R. A. and D. Schulman. 1995a. "Public Perceptions of Global Warming." *Climate Change* 1(29):1–33.

———. 1995b. *Willingness to Pay for Water Saving Household Appliances: A Report to Association Urban Water Agencies.* Los Angeles: University of California, Los Angeles, Center for Statistics, Working Paper.

Berk, R. A. and L. W. Sherman. 1988. "Police Responses to Family Violence Incidents: An Analysis of an Experimental Design With Incomplete Randomization." *Journal of the American Statistical Association* 83:70–76.

Berk, R. A., B. Western, and R. Weiss. 1995. "Statistical Inference for Apparent Populations." Pp. 421–58 in *Sociological Methodology 1991,* edited by P. Marsden. Washington, DC: American Sociological Association.

Bertram, E., M. Blackman, K. Sharp, and P. Andreas. 1996. *Drug War Politics: The Price of Denial.* Berkeley: University of California Press.

Besharov, D., Germanis, P., and Rossi, P. H. 1997. *Evaluating Welfare Reform: A Guide for Scholars and Practitioners.* College Park, MD: Welfare Reform Academy, University of Maryland.

Bickman, L., A. R. Guthrie, M. Foster, E. W. Lambert, W. T. Summerfelt, C. Breda, and C. Heflinger. 1995. *Managed Care in Mental Health: The Fort Bragg Experiment.* New York: Plenum Press.

Bickman, L. and M. S. Salzer, eds. 1997. "Measuring Quality in Mental Health Services." *Evaluation Review* 3(21):285–416.

Bickman, L., W. T. Summerfelt, and K. Noser. 1997. "Comparative Outcomes of Emotionally Disturbed Children and Adolescents in a System of Services and Usual Care." *Psychiatric Services* 12(48):1543–48.

Bloom, D., H. Kopp, D. Long, and D. Politt. 1991. *Implementing a Welfare Initiative to Improve School Attendance Among Teenage Parents.* New York: Manpower Demonstration Research.

Boruch, R. F. 1997. *Randomized Experiments for Planning and Evaluation.* Thousand Oaks, CA: Sage.

Boudett, K. P. and D. Friedlander. 1997. "Does Mandatory Basic Education Improve Achievement Test Scores of AFDC Recipients: A Reanalysis of Data From the California GAIN Program." *Evaluation Review* 5(21):568–88.

Bowden, R. J. and D. A. Turkington. 1984. *Instrumental Variables.* Cambridge: Cambridge University Press.

Boyd, E., K. Hamner, and R. A. Berk. 1996. "Motivated by Hatred or Prejudice: Categorization of Hate-Motivated Crimes in Two Police Divisions." *American Sociological Review* 4(30):819–50.

Briggs, J. and F. D. Peat. 1989. *Turbulent Mirror.* New York: Harper and Row.

California Department of Corrections. 1997. *A Report on the Inmate Classification System.* Sacramento: Author.

Campbell, D. T. and A. Erlebacher. 1970. "How Regression Artifacts in Quasi-Experimental Evaluations Make Compensatory Education Look Harmful." Pp. 185–210 in *Compensatory Education: A National Debate,* edited by J. Hellmuth. New York: Brunner/Mazel.

Carson, R. 1955. *Silent Spring.* New York: Bantam.

Chen, H. 1990. *Theory-Driven Evaluations.* Newbury Park, CA: Sage.

Chen, H. and R. H. Rossi. 1980. "The Multi-Goal, Theory-Driven Approach to Evaluation: A Model Linking Basic and Applied Social Science." *Social Forces* 59(1): 106–22.

Cicirelli, V. G., et al. 1969. *The Impact of Head Start.* Athens: Westinghouse Learning Corporation and Ohio State University.

Cochran, W. 1983. *Planning and Analysis of Observational Studies.* New York: John Wiley.

Coleman, J., et al. 1967. *Equality of Educational Opportunity.* Washington, DC: Government Printing Office.

Conant, James B. 1959. *The American High School Today.* New York: McGraw-Hill.

Cook, T. and D. Campbell. 1979. *Quasi-Experimentation.* Chicago: Rand McNally.

Cook, T. D., H. Cooper, D. S. Cordray, H. Hartmann, L. V. Hedges, R. J. Light, T. A. Louis, and F. Mosteller, eds. 1992. *Meta-Analysis for Explanation: A Casebook.* New York: Russell Sage Foundation.

Cook, P. J., J. Ludwig, and D. Hemenway. 1997. "The Gun Debate's New Mythical Number: How Many Defensive Uses Per Year?" *Policy Analysis and Management* 3(16):463–69.

Cook, T., et al. 1975. *Sesame Street Revisited.* New York: Russell Sage.

Cronbach, L. J. 1975. "Five Decades of Controversy Over Mental Testing." *American Psychologist* 30(1):1–14.

———. 1982. *Designing Evaluations of Educational and Social Programs.* Menlo Park, CA: Jossey-Bass.

Cronbach, L. J. and Associates. 1980. *Towards Reform of Program Evaluation.* Menlo Park, CA: Jossey-Bass.

de Gruijl, F. R. 1995. "Impacts of a Projected Depletion of the Ozone Layer." *Consequences: The Natural Implications of Environmental Change* 2(1):12–21.

Deutscher, I. 1977. "Toward Avoiding the Goal Trap in Evaluation Research." Pp. 221–38 in *Readings in Evaluation Research,* edited by E. Caro. New York: Russell Sage.

Dobson, M., D. A. Grayson, R. P. Marshall, B. I. O'Toole, S. R. Leeder, and R. Schureck. 1996. "The Impact of a Counseling Service Program on the Psychosocial Morbidity of Australian Vietnam Veterans." *Evaluation Review* 6(20):670–94.

Duke, D. D. and P. G. Breswick. 1997. "Industry Compliance With Storm Water Pollution Prevention Regulations: The Case of Transportation Industry Facilities in California and the Los Angeles Region." *Journal of the American Water Resources Association* 4(33):825–38.

Edgington, E. S. 1987. *Randomization Tests.* 2nd ed. New York: Marcel Dekker.

Edin, K. and L. Lein. 1997. *Making Ends Meet: How Single Mothers Survive Welfare and Low-Wage Work.* New York: Russell Sage Foundation.

Ericksen, E. R. and J. B. Kadane. 1985. "Estimating the Population in a Census Year: 1980 and Beyond." *Journal of the American Statistical Association* 80:98–131.

Esbensen, F., E. P. Deschenes, R. E. Vogel, J. West, K. Arbott, and L. Harris. 1996. "Active Parental Consent in School-Based Research: An Examination of Ethical and Methodological Issues. *Evaluation Review* 6(20):737–53.

Everitt, B. S. 1984. *An Introduction to Latent Variable Models.* New York: Chapman Hall.

Fairweather, G. and L. G. Tornatzky. 1977. *Experimental Methods for Social Policy Research.* New York: Pergamon Press.

Franke, R. H. 1979. "The Hawthorne Experiments: Review." *American Sociological Review* 44(5):861–67.

Franke, R. H. and J. D. Kaul. 1978. "The Hawthorne Experiments: First Statistical Interpretation." *American Sociological Review* 43(5):623–43.

Franker, T. and R. Maynard. 1987. "The Adequacy of Comparison Group Designs for Evaluations of Employment-Related Programs." *Journal of Human Resources* 22:194–227.

Frederick, K. D. 1995. "America's Water Supply: Stratus and Prospects for the Future." *Consequences: The Nature and Implications of Environmental Change* 1(1):13–23.

Freedman, D. A. 1987. "As Others See Us: A Case Study of Path Analysis." *Journal of Educational Statistics* 12(2), entire issue.

Freedman, D. A. 1991. "Statistical Models and Shoe Leather." Pp. 291–313 in *Sociological Methodology,* edited by P. Marsden. Oxford: Basil Blackwell.

Freedman, D. A., R. Pisani, and R. Purves, 1998. *Statistics.* New York: Norton.

Freedman, D. A. and K. W. Wachter. 1996. "Planning for the Census in the Year 2000." *Evaluation Review* 4(20):355–77.

Freedman, D. A. and H. Zeisel. 1988. "Cancer and Risk Assessment: From Mouse to Man." *Statistical Science* 3:1–27.

Fuller, W. A. 1987. *Measurement Error Models.* New York: John Wiley.

Gans, H. J. 1995. *The War Against the Poor: The Underclass and Antipoverty Policy.* New York: Basic Books.

Geisel, M. S., R. Roll, and R. S. Wettick, Jr. 1969. "The Effectiveness of State and Local Regulation of Handguns: A Statistical Analysis." *Duke Law Journal* (August): 647–76.

General Accounting Office. 1986. *Teenage Pregnancy: 500,000 Births a Year but Few Tested Programs.* Washington, DC: Author.

Glantz, F. B., Rodda, D., Cutler, M. J., Rhodes, W., and Wrobel, M. 1997. *Early Childhood and Child Care Study: Profile of Participants in the CACFP. Volume I. Final Report.* Alexandria, VA: U.S. Department of Agriculture, Food and Consumer Service.

Glass, G. V., B. McGraw, and M. L. Smith. 1981. *Meta-Analysis in Social Research.* Beverly Hills, CA: Sage.

Gleick, P. H. 1993. *Water in Crisis: A Guide to the World's Fresh Water Resources.* New York: Oxford University Press.

Good, P. 1993. *Permutation Tests: A Practical Guide to Resampling Methods for Testing Hypotheses.* New York: Springer-Verlag.

Goodman, S. N. and R. Royall. 1988. "Evidence and Scientific Research." *American Journal of Public Health* 78(12):1568–75.

Gramlich, E. M. and R. Koshel. 1975. *Educational Performance Contracting.* Washington, DC: Brookings Institution.

Guba, E. and Y. Lincoln. 1981. *Effective Evaluation.* Menlo Park, CA: Jossey-Bass.

Gueron, J. and E. Pauly. 1991. *From Welfare to Work.* New York: Russell Sage.

Guttentag, M. and E. Struening, eds. 1975. *Handbook of Evaluation Research.* 2 vols. Beverly Hills, CA: Sage.

Handler, J. F. 1995. *The Poverty of Welfare Reform.* New Haven, CT: Yale University Press.

Harrington, M. 1962. *The Other America.* New York: Macmillan.

Hausman, J. A. and D. A. Wise. 1985. *Social Experimentation.* Chicago: University of Chicago Press.

Heckman, J. and R. Robb. 1985. "Alternative Methods for Evaluating the Impact of Interventions." In *Longitudinal Analysis of Labor Market Data,* edited by J. J. Heckman and B. Singer. New York: Cambridge University Press.

———. 1986. "Alternative Methods for Solving the Problem of Selection Bias in Evaluating the Impact of Treatments on Outcomes." In *Drawing Inferences From Self-Selected Samples,* edited by H. Wainer. New York: Springer-Verlag.

Hedges, L. V. and I. Olkin. 1988. *Statistical Methods for Meta-Analysis.* New York: Academic Press.

Heilman, J. G. 1980. "Paradigmatic Choices in Evaluation Methodology." *Evaluation Review* 4(5): 693–712.

Hemenway, D. 1997. "The Myth of Millions of Annual Self-Defense Gun Uses: A Case Study of Survey Overestimation of Rare Events." *Change* 3(10):6–10.

Holland, R. W. 1986. "Statistics and Causal Inference." *Journal of the American Statistical Association* 81:945–60.

Holland, R. W. and D. B. Rubin. 1988. "Causal Inference in Retrospective Studies." *Evaluation Review* 12(3):203–31.

Intergovernmental Panel on Climate Change. 1997. *Special Report on the Regional Impacts of Climate Change.* London: Cambridge University Press.

Kadzin, A. E. 1982. *Single Case Research Designs.* New York: Oxford University Press.

Kershaw, D. and J. Fair. 1976. *The New Jersey Income Maintenance Experiment.* New York: Academic Press.

Kessler, D. A. and S. Duncan. 1996. "The Impact of Community Policing in Four Houston Neighborhoods." *Evaluation Review* 6(20):627–69.

Kish, L. 1965. *Survey Sampling.* New York: John Wiley.

———. 1987. *Statistical Design for Research.* New York: John Wiley.

Kleck, G. and M. Gertz. 1995. "Armed Resistance to Crime: The Prevalence and Nature of Self-Defense with a Gun." *Journal of Criminal Law and Criminology* 1(37): 23–38.

Kmenta, J. 1971. *Elements of Econometrics.* New York: Macmillan.

Koegel, P., M. A. Burnam, and S. C. Morton. 1996. "Enumerating the Homeless: Alternative Strategies and Their Consequences." *Evaluation Review* 4(20):378–403.

Krug, A. S. 1967. "The Relationship Between Firearm Licensing Laws and Crime Rates." *Congressional Record* 113(July 25):2000.60(64.

LaLonde, R. 1986. "Evaluating the Econometric Evaluations of Training Programs with Experimental Data." *American Economics Review* 76:604–20.

Leamer, E. E. 1978. *Specification Searches.* New York: John Wiley.

Lenihan, K. 1976. *Opening the Second Gate.* Washington, DC: Government Printing Office.

Levy, P. S. and S. Lemeshow. 1991. *Sampling of Populations: Methods and Applications.* New York: John Wiley.

Lewis, D. A., T. Pavkov, H. Rosenberg, S. Reed, A. Lurigio, Z. Kalifon, B. Johnson, and S. Riger. 1987. *State Hospitalization Utilization in Chicago.* Evanston, IL: Center for Urban Affairs and Policy Research.

Lewis, O. 1965. *La Vida.* New York: Random House.

Liebow, E. 1967. *Tally's Corner.* Boston: Little, Brown.

Lipsey, M. W. 1992. "Juvenile Delinquency Treatment: A Meta-Analysis Inquiry Into the Variability of Effects." In *Meta-Analysis for Explanation: A Casebook,* edited by T. D. Cook, H. Cooper, D. S. Cordray, H. Hartmann, L. V. Hedges, R. J. Light, T. A. Louis, and F. Mosteller. New York: Russell Sage.

Lord, E. M. 1980. *Applications of Item Response Theory to Practical Testing Problems.* Hillsdale, NJ: Lawrence Erlbaum.

Lord, F. and H. Novick. 1968. *Statistical Theories of Mental Test Scores.* Reading, MA: Addison-Wesley.

Luepker, R. V., C. L. Perry, S. M. McKinlay, P. R. Nader, G. S. Parcel, E. J. Stone, L. S. Webber, J. P. Elder, H. A. Feldman, C. C. Johnson, S. H. Kelder, and M. Wu. In press. "Outcomes of a Field Trial to Improve Children's Dietary Patterns and Physical Activity: The Child and Adolescent Trial for Cardiovascular Health (CATCH)." *Journal of the American Medical Association.*

Mathematica Policy Research. 1980. *Job Corps Evaluated.* Princeton, NJ: Mathematica.

Maynard, R. A. and R. J. Murnane. 1979. "The Effects of the Negative Income Tax on School Performance." *Journal of Human Resources* 141:463–76.

Mensh, I. N. and J. Henry. 1953. "Direct Observation and Psychological Tests in Anthropological Field Work." *American Anthropology* 55(4):461–80.

Meyers, M. K., B. Glaser, and K. MacDonald. 1998. "On the Front Lines of Welfare Delivery: Are Workers Implementing Welfare Reform?" *Journal of Policy Analysis and Management* 1(17):1–22.

Milavsky, J. R., H. H. Stipp, R. C. Kessler, and W. S. Rubens. 1982. *Television and Aggression: A Panel Study.* New York: Academic Press.

Murray, S. A. 1980. *The National Evaluation of the PUSH for Excellence Project* (manuscript). Washington, DC: American Institutes for Research.

Murray, W. A. 1981. *Final Report: Evaluation of Cities in School Program* (manuscript). Washington, DC: American Institutes for Research.

Nathan, R., F. C. Doolittle, and Associates. 1983. *The Consequences of Cuts.* Princeton, NJ: Princeton Urban and Regional Research Center.

Nordhaus, W. D. 1994. *Managing the Global Commons: The Economics of Climate Change.* Cambridge, MA: MIT Press.

Office of Science and Technology. 1997. *Climate Change: State of Knowledge.* Washington, DC: Executive Office of the President.

Patton, M. Q. 1997. *Utilization Focused Evaluation.* 3rd ed. Thousand Oaks, CA: Sage.

Pinkerton, S. D. and P. R. Abramson. 1996. "Implications for Increased Infectivity in Early-Stage HIV Infection: An Application of a Bernoulli-Process Model of HIV Infection." *Evaluation Review* 5(20):516–40.

Pollard, W. E. 1986. *Bayesian Statistics for Evaluation Research.* Beverly Hills, CA: Sage.

Pratt, J. W. and R. Schlaifer. 1984. "On the Nature and Discovery of Structure." *Journal of the American Statistical Association* 79(1):9–21.

Raizen, S. and P. H. Rossi. 1981. *Program Evaluation in Education: When? How? To What Ends?* Washington, DC: National Academy Press.

Reiss, A. E. 1971. *The Police and the Public.* New Haven, CT: Yale University Press.

Riccio, J., D. Friedlander, and S. Freedman. 1994. *GAIN: Benefits, Costs and the Three-Year Impacts of a Welfare-to-Work Program.* New York: Demonstration Research Corporation.

Riis, J. A. 1890. *How the Other Half Lives.* New York: Scribner.

Riley, K. J. 1995. *Snow Job? The War Against International Cocaine Trafficking.* New Brunswick, NJ: Transaction.

Robertson, L. S. 1980. "Crash Involvement of Teenaged Drivers When Driver Education Is Eliminated From High School." *American Journal of Public Health* 70(161):599–603.

Robins, P. K., et al. 1980. *A Guaranteed Annual Income: Evidence From a Social Experiment.* New York: Academic Press.

Rosenbaum, P. R. 1995. *Observational Studies.* New York: Springer-Verlag.

Rosenbaum, P. R. and D. B. Rubin. 1985. "The Bias Due to Incomplete Matching." *Biometrics* 41:103–16.

Rossi, P. H. 1978. "Issues in the Evaluation of Human Services Delivery." *Evaluation Quarterly* 214:573–99.

———. 1987. "The Iron Law of Evaluation and Other Metallic Rules." Pp. 3–20 in *Research in Social Problems and Public Policy,* Vol. 4, edited by J. Miller and M. Lewis. Greenwich, CT: JAI.

———. 1994. "Troubling Families: Family Homelessness in America." *American Behavioral Scientist* 37(January 1994):342–95.

———. 1998a. Evaluating Community Development Programs: Problems and Prospects. In *Community Development Programs,* edited by R. Ferguson and W. Dickens. Washington, DC: Brookings Institution.

———. 1998b. *Feeding the Poor: Five Federal Nutrition Programs.* Washington, DC: American Enterprise Institute.

Rossi, P. H., R. A. Berk, and B. K. Eidson. 1974. *The Roots of Urban Discontent.* New York: John Wiley.

Rossi, P. H., R. Berk, and K. Lenihan. 1980. *Money, Work and Crime.* New York: Academic Press.

Rossi, P. H. and B. Biddle. 1966. *The New Media and Education.* Chicago: Aldine.

Rossi, P. H. and R. Dentler. 1961. *The Politics of Urban Renewal: The Chicago Findings.* New York: Free Press.

Rossi, P. H., G. Fisher, and G. Willis. 1986. *The Condition of the Homeless of Chicago.* Amherst, MA, and Chicago: Social and Demographic Research Institute, University of Massachusetts, and NORC (A Social Science Research Institute, University of Chicago).

Rossi, P. H. and H. Freeman. 1993. *Evaluation: A Systematic Approach.* 5th ed. Thousand Oaks, CA: Sage.

Rossi, P. H. and K. Lyall. 1974. *Reforming Public Welfare.* New York: Russell Sage.

Rossi, P. H., J. D. Wright, G. Fisher, and G. Willis. 1987. "The Urban Homeless: Estimating Compostion and Size." *Science* 235:1336–41.

Rossi, P. H., J. D. Wright, E. Weber-Burdin, and J. Pereira. 1983. *Victims of the Environment: Loss From Natural Hazards in the United States, 1970–1980.* New York: Academic Press.

Rothschild, B. J. 1996. "How Bountiful Are Ocean Fisheries?" *Consequences: The Nature and Implications of Environmental Change* 1(2):14–24.

Rubin, D. B. 1977. "Assignment of Treatment Group on the Basis of a Covariate." *Journal of Education Statistics* 2:1–26.

———. 1978. "Bayesian Inference for Causal Effects: The Role of Randomization." *The Annals of Statistics* 6:34–58.

———. 1986. "Which Ifs Have Causal Answers?" *Journal of the American Statistical Association* 81:961–62.

Sarndal, C.-E., B. Swensson, and J. Wretman. 1992. *Model Assisted Survey Sampling.* New York: Springer-Verlag.

Scriven, M. 1972. "Pros and Cons About Goal-Free Evaluation." *Evaluation Comment* 311:1–4.

Sechrest, L. and M. Walsh. 1997. "Dogma or Data: Bragging Rights." *American Psychologist* 2(52):536–40.

Seitz, S. T. 1972. "Firearms, Homicide and Gun Control Effectiveness." *Law and Society Review* 6(May):595–613.

Sherman, L. W. and E. G. Cohn. 1989. "The Impact of Research on Legal Policy: The Minneapolis Domestic Violence Experiment." *Law and Society Review* 23(1): 117–45.

Sinclair, U. 1906. *The Jungle.* New York: Doubleday.

Smith, V. K., W. H. Desvousges, A. Fisher, and E. R. Johnson. 1987. *Communicating Radon Risk Effectively: A Mid-Course Evaluation* (Publication #EPA-230-07-87-029). Washington, DC: Environmental Protection Agency.

Spitzer, R. J. 1995. *The Politics of Gun Control.* Chatham, NJ: Chatham House.

Steinbeck, John. 1939. *The Grapes of Wrath.* New York: Viking.

Struyk, R. and M. Bendick. 1981. *Housing Vouchers for the Poor: Lessons From a National Experiment.* Washington, DC: Urban Institute.

Suchman, E. 1967. *Evaluation Research.* New York: Russell Sage.

Sudman, S. 1976. *Applied Sampling.* New York: Academic Press.

Teasley, C. E. 1996. "Where's the Best Medicine? The Hospital Rating Game." *Evaluation Review* 5(20):558–79.

Thompson, M. 1980. *Cost-Benefit Analysis.* Beverly Hills, CA: Sage.

Treno, A. J. and H. D. Holder. 1997. "Special Issue: Evaluation Design for a Community Trial to Reduce Alcohol-Involved Trauma: An Environmental Approach to Prevention." *Evaluation Review* 2(21):133–277.

Trochim, W. M. K. 1984. *Research Design for Program Evaluation: The Regression Discontinuity Approach.* Beverly Hills, CA: Sage.

U.S. Conference of Mayors. 1987. *The Continuing Growth of Hunger, Homelessness, and Poverty in U.S. Cities: 1987.* Washington, DC: Author.

Van Ryzin, G. G. 1996. "The Impact of Resident Management on Resident's Satisfaction With Public Housing." *Evaluation Review* 4(20):485–506.

Wardwell, W. L. 1979. "Comment on Kaul and Franke." *American Sociological Review* 44(5):858–61.

Weiss, C. 1972. *Evaluation Research.* Englewood Cliffs, NJ: Prentice Hall.

———. 1997. "How Can Theory-Based Evaluation Make Headway?" *Evaluation Review* 4(21):501–24.

Wentland, E. J. and K. W. Smith. 1993. *Survey Responses: An Evaluation of Their Validity.* New York: Academic Press.

Wholey, J. S. 1977. "Evaluability Assessment." Pp. 49–56 in *Evaluation Research Methods,* edited by L. Putnam. Beverly Hills, CA: Sage.

Wright, J. D., P. H. Rossi, and K. Daly. 1983. *Under the Gun: Weapons, Crime and Violence in America.* New York: Aldine.

Ziegler, E. and S. Muenchow. 1992. *Head Start: The Inside Story of America's Most Successful Educational Experiment.* New York: Basic Books.

Index

119

About the Authors

Richard A. Berk is a Professor in the Departments of Statistics and Sociology at the University of California at Los Angeles and Director of the UCLA Statistical Consulting Center. He has been involved in evaluation research for 25 years as a practitioner, as a contributor to evaluation research methods, and as an editor of the *Evaluation Review.* Current evaluation projects include work with the California Department of Corrections on the their inmate classification and placement procedures, with the Los Angeles Department of Water and Power on their water conservation and demand management initiatives, and with UCLA atmospheric scientists on the application of statistical tools to evaluate computer simulation models employed to simulate short-term meteorological and air quality in the Los Angeles Basin. Professor Berk has authored 12 books and over 150 article and book chapters. He is a member of the American Statistical Association and a Fellow in the American Association for the Advancement of Science. He was awarded the Paul F. Lazarsfeld award by the American Sociological Association for his contributions to sociological research methods.

Peter H. Rossi is Rice Professor Emeritus of Sociology and Director Emeritus of the Social and Demographic Research Institute at the University of Massachusetts at Amherst. He has been on the faculties

University. From 1960 to 1967, he was Director of the National Opinion Research Center at the University of Chicago. He is a past president of the American Sociological Association and was the 1985 recipient of the Common Wealth Award for contributions to sociology. He has received awards from the Evaluation Research Society, the Eastern Evaluation Research Society, and the Policy Studies Association for his contributions to evaluation research methodology. His recent books include *Evaluation: A Systematic Approach* (1993, with Howard Freeman), *Of Human Bonding* (1990, with Alice S. Rossi), *Down and Out in America* (1989), *Just Punishments* (1997, with R. A. Berk), and *Feeding the Poor* (1998). He has served as editor of the *American Journal of Sociology* and *Social Science Research*. He has been elected a Fellow of the American Academy of Arts and Sciences and of the American Association for the Advancement of Science.